The Chaos
Conundrum

Aaron John Gulyas

Starhawk
Publishing

The Chaos Conundrum
Copyright © 2013 Aaron John Gulyas (www.ajgulyas.com)

All photos are © Aaron John Gulyas.

Cover design by Paul Kimball; artwork by Mac Tonnies.

ISBN: 978-0-9916975-7-1

Published by Starhawk Publishing.
www.starhawkpublishing.com
19 Sherbrooke Drive, Halifax, NS, Canada B3M 1P5

Essays on UFOs, Ghosts &
Other High Strangeness in our
Non-Rational & Atemporal
World

Table of Contents

ACKNOWLEDGMENTS

Okay – this one was a bit weird to work on, as may become apparent when you read it. What started out as a collection of essays exploring the cultural aspects of the paranormal became a bit more experiential once I began writing, which definitely made it more personal. While it was sometimes awkward to sever the scholarly detachment with which I've been shielding myself for 20-odd years, it was rewarding. Thanks, of course, to Paul Kimball, my editor and publisher at Starhawk Publishing, for the opportunity to do so in a relatively low-stress environment, and the guidance he provided during the process.

Also, Paul deserves the credit for what might be the most fun I've had on the internet in years when he and I spent an hour in a comment thread on Facebook undertaking a real-time *Mystery Science Theatre*-style riffing of exopolitics figure Ed Komarek's appearance on Richard Dolan's radio program back in April 2013 (there is more about Komarek and his particular viewpoint later in these pages).

My intellectual debts in this book are many. Andy and Shelly Gage have been friends for over twenty years, and in that time have shaped much of my thinking about the traditional view of ghosts and hauntings.

My interest about hauntology, atemporality, and the like can be traced back to writer Warren Ellis's work and, of course, that of Jacques Derrida, whom well-meaning faculty forced me to read in graduate school.

My ideas about the paranormal have come from too many sources to quickly identify, but as you read this book, you'll probably be able to spot them. One important one was a Reverend Barlow who, in 1990, responded thoughtfully and open-mindedly to my question in confirmation class about UFOs and the Bible. Looking back, that's probably the earliest starting point for a lot of the ideas in here.

As I've mentioned online, in these pages, and in the acknowledgements section of *Extraterrestrials and the American Zeitgeist*, the work of Paul Kimball and the late Mac Tonnies was paramount in getting me interested in what was (and in many ways still is) a paranormal scene that had stagnated. Nick Redfern, Greg Bishop, Walter Bosley, Tony Morrill, and Micah Hanks have helped keep that interest active enough for me to want to write on. Extra thanks, of course, to Nick for penning the foreword to this collection.

I have also benefitted from a rapidly changing world of publishing and, more broadly, of disseminating ideas. Small presses like Starhawk and others are the vanguard when it comes to getting new ideas and approaches into the hands of the reading public. Whether on a computer screen, e-reader, or paper, the written word still carries weight. New production and distribution channels will help ensure that those words represent a vast diversity of options, views, and ideas.

Finally, and most importantly, thanks and love as always to Cindy and Matthew for putting up with my nonsense.

Aaron John Gulyas
14 November, 2013

FOREWORD

By Nick Redfern

Aaron Gulyas' *The Chaos Conundrum* is a thoughtful, and thought-provoking, compilation of papers on a wide variety of paranormal phenomena. Or, as it's collectively known in circles where the unusual is typically the usual: profoundly weird stuff. A cursory glance at the titles of the essays, and their attendant subject matters, might make some readers assume they are stand-alone pieces with no connecting or unifying parts. Well, those souls would be wrong. Actually, they would be dead wrong.

The connection is not so much the issues and topics that Gulyas places under his supernatural microscope. Rather, it is the fact that the essays all invite us to do one thing: address and consider alternative theories, paradigms, and ideas to those that the established figures of the paranormal would prefer we adhere to.

Of course, there are some who will only accept the invite if they are dragged kicking and screaming like a little kid about to have a tooth removed. Too bad, as those closed-minded, belief-driven ostriches could learn a great deal from delving deep into *The Chaos Conundrum*. For some, unfortunately, extracting head from sand is not that easy. Since you're now reading these words, I presume – and sincerely hope – that does not apply to you.

Before I get to the meat of the matter, I should note that Gulyas has a fine writing style; it's one that is various parts sly humor, engaging wit, imagination, and the ability to craft and weave a fine, gripping story. This alone makes *The Chaos Conundrum* a book that not only massively informs, but which highly entertains, too.

So, with that all said, what do we get from reading Gulyas' book? Let's take a look. The book is not exactly an autobiography, nor is that the intention of the author. It does, however, contain several chapters that are, at the very least, semi-autobiographical, in the sense that Gulyas uses personal experiences to help get his points across. And they are points very well made.

As people familiar with my work will know, I'm not overly interested in the phenomenon of ghosts. In fact, it's fair to say that the words "could," "not," "care," and "less" spring to mind. The primary reason for my bias is not so much the topic itself, but the fact that the investigation of the subject is so deeply enmeshed in tiresome predictability.

Thankfully, Gulyas does not make me want to punch the wall by talking endlessly about night-vision equipment or regaling us with cries of "what the hell was that?!" We get way too much of that on the many terrible shows that pass for "reality TV." Nope: instead Gulyas held my attention by digging into the greatly intriguing world of archaeoacoustics.

Say what?

Well, this is a fascinating theory, to say the least. I won't give the game away, since I'm here to tell you a bit about the book, not spill the entire can of beans. But I will say that Gulyas introduces us to a realm of research that offers potentials that are near-mind-blowing. And I never once got bored reading about it!

Roswell also gets the Gulyas treatment. Not so much from the perspective of what happened, however, but with regard to how ufology has made the infamous 1947 event the one upon which the subject of UFOs stands. Granted, this may not have been done deliberately or consciously. But that doesn't take away the fact that Roswell defines ufology, like it or not. Well, Gulyas doesn't like it.

He correctly notes there are other cases out there that are of prime importance and which may surpass Roswell in terms of presenting evidence that we have been visited by... well, something. Gulyas' Roswell essay is a fine one that reveals much of what is wrong about ufology. It also shows why belief has actually limited – rather than expanded – what should pass for investigative research into the puzzling event.

Still on the matter of UFOs, Gulyas plunges deep into the heart of the thorny theory that the UFO phenomenon has demonic origins. I know much about this, as I wrote a book on the subject: *Final Events*. I don't, however, personally adhere to the theory at all. Rather, my book was a study of how and why a think-tank-style group in government came to that conclusion.

I have seen the demonic angle dismissed out of hand by the Extraterrestrial Hypothesis brigade. And I have seen it endorsed by believers who try and terrify people into accepting it, lest they suffer a never-ending afterlife burning in Hell. Fortunately, Gulyas addresses the matter in a very refreshing fashion.

There's no outright dismissal of the type shown by those ufologists who won't even give the idea a second thought. And, thankfully, there's no banging on the pulpit. Instead, we are treated to an excellent paper from our author that looks at the pros and cons of the theory, but without any attendant, manipulative, controlling, fear-based agenda.

Gulyas' study of the crop circle puzzle is a highly entertaining and amusing one. It also introduces us to something that many of us who investigate paranormal topics experience: namely, the way in which the phenomena seem to interact with the investigators on a deeply personal, ever-increasing basis.

Becoming a target of the phenomena – or, at least, feeling manipulated by it – can be daunting to some, but Gulyas handles it well. Rather than denying the presence, or running away from it, he applies much thought and time to understanding what's afoot and why.

We also get a good look at what Gulyas thinks about certain people in the field of ufology and conspiracy research. Top of the list are Bill Cooper, Gray Barker, Jim Moseley, and those attached to the field of exopolitics. Gulyas, to his credit, tells it as he sees it. Some of it is good. Some of it is not. But it all serves to demonstrate that people are highly complex animals with varying agendas. Sometimes, those agendas have left major marks on the field of ufology and conspiracy research.

There's much more I could tell you about *The Chaos Conundrum*. But I won't. Instead, I invite you to indulge yourself in the work of a man who has made a major contribution to the domain of paranormal research, writing and observation.

Read it, consider it, and learn from it. Just don't be an ostrich about it.

Nick Redfern is the author of many books, including *Monster Diary, Contactees, The Real Men in Black, Three Men Seeking Monsters*, and *There's Something in the Woods*.

Introduction
THE NON-RATIONAL
& THE ATEMPORAL

Once, a few years ago, I was in the position of having to teach an introductory "Critical Thinking" course. One of the most interesting areas that I covered, which was a bit difficult for the students to grasp, was the distinction between ideas, claims, or arguments that were *irrational*, as opposed to those that were *non-rational*.

Irrational ideas are those which break the standard rules of logic as they have been handed down to us through the thought and philosophy of Western Civilization since the time of the Greeks. Irrational claims are unsupported by the available evidence. If a salesperson presents you with a car that has been smashed by a train and attempts to convince you that any damage you notice is all in your head, that's an irrational claim which is clearly refuted by the mass of twisted metal in front of you.

The non-rational is more difficult to describe or assess. Miracles are non-rational; God is non-rational. Irrational arguments break the rules of proof and logic. Non-rational arguments exist in a universe which operates under different rules. There are times when that universe has no discernible rules at all. The paranormal begins in this non-rational universe, although as we'll see, it may not end there.

Sometimes, as our understanding of the universe expands, phenomena cross the line from non-rational to rational; our "rulebook" expands along with our knowledge. Despite all of the great strides we have made over the course of human history in terms of expanding our knowledge, there are questions which remain outside that rulebook. Ghosts, extraterrestrial life, "alien abductions" – all of these seem amenable to our rationalist guidelines, but like a round peg in a square hole they never quite fit. They always stay uncomfortably across the line that separates the rational from the non-rational. Of course, the situation is complicated when proponents of a particular theory about the paranormal use the language of rationality – or emotive barrages of irrationality – to press their points of view.

As someone who has, for most of his life, been interested in the numinous and non-rational, the constellation of events, phenomena, and ideas known as "the paranormal" has always exerted a strong pull on me. As a child, I remember re-runs of the television series *In Search Of...*, and being enthralled by Leonard Nimoy spinning tales of the Bermuda Triangle, ghosts, Bigfoot, psychics, Atlantis, Ogopogo, the 1908 Tunguska explosion, and dozens of other topics that occupied a place just beyond polite conversation at the dinner table.[1] But while I was fascinated by all of these things, it was flying saucers that really seemed to speak to me. Perhaps this was not surprising given my love of *Star Trek*, *Star Wars*, *Doctor Who* and other forms of science fiction and space opera. My interest in paranoia and conspiracy theories emerged in the mid 1990s, as the dawn of *The X-Files* coincided with my arrival at college and my first access to the vast amount of information on the burgeoning Internet. I was overwhelmed and excited.

---

[1] *In Search of...*, Hosted by Leonard Nimoy, Alan Landsburg Productions, 1977 – 1982, 30 min. per episode, 144 episodes.

Before dismissing me as a tin-foil hat wearing super-geek turned crackpot, however, remember that this was all new to me. I watched Mulder, Scully, the Lone Gunmen, and the Cigarette Smoking Man meander through their conspiracies and then – wonder of wonders – I discovered that these conspiracies might actually be real! I read the writings of John Lear and William Cooper, and combed through Usenet groups and archived posts from the Paranet forums where I read things like this:

> The EBEs have a genetic disorder in that their digestive system is atrophied and not functional. Some speculate that they were involved in some type of accident or nuclear war, or that they are possibly on the back side of an evolutionary genetic curve. In order to sustain themselves, they use an enzyme or hormonal secretion obtained from the tissue they extract from humans and animals.[2]

Intrigued, I went deeper, looking at things like the Krill papers and Val Valerian's MATRIX collections. I listened to the *Paranet Continuum*, and Art Bell's *Coast to Coast AM* and *Dreamland* shows, on the Radio. I read every paranormal magazine and website I could get my hands on.

---

[2] John Lear, *The UFO Coverup*, www.sacred-texts.com/ufo/coverup.htm. During the late 1980s and early 1990s, John Lear, a pilot and son of the famous inventor of the Lear Jet, came forward with what he claimed was the truth about UFOs and the extraterrestrial presence on Earth. He became a frequent guest on conspiracy-oriented talk radio, until his claims became so outlandish, encompassing virtually every conspiracy theory he could find, that he was discredited to all but the smallest group of true believers. For the story of Wild Bill Cooper, you will have wait until chapter 5!

As the line blurred between paranormal and paranoid, I explored the thought behind the so-called "patriot" and "militia" movements of the end of the century. The more of this material I read, the more I realized that – in some cases - I actually had a deeper and more detailed knowledge of these topics than the paranormal journalists. At the time, I attributed this to my stellar knowledge and deep insight. Over the years, however, I have come to a different conclusion.

There just is not enough substance to most tales of the paranormal. With nearly all of the major stories and theories, from EVP to Roswell to chupacabras (and all the weird points in between), there comes a wall beyond which one simply cannot go any further. And so, after spending a considerable amount of time dealing with many of these paranormal topics, one becomes familiar not only with the basic story, but with the various alternatives to that story, including any number of viewpoints designed to debunk them. Despite investigations into paranormal and conspiracy topics often reaching some sort of logical (if often unsatisfying) conclusion, the stories continue on in their particular subcultures as well as in the wider popular culture.

Because of this continuity, various fields of the paranormal begin to resemble a kind of remix culture. Bits and pieces get reused and re-purposed over the years, blended into newer stories and retold over and over again. This realization came to me when I was looking at a paranormal-focused message board on the web one day. A new member had asked others what they knew about the mythical joint human-alien underground base that supposedly existed at Dulce, New Mexico. Stories of this base had been a mainstay of conspiratorial paranormality in the 1990s. By the early 21st century these stories had been convincingly shown to be Air Force disinformation by books like Mark Pilkington's *Mirage Men* and Greg Bishop's (superior, in my opinion) *Project Beta*.[3]

Despite the logical and supported explanations presented by the likes of Pilkington and Bishop, however, the idea of a secret subterranean base at Dulce has persisted. This incident led me to believe that my explorations of the paranormal would, in all likelihood, not result in some sort of revelation or truth behind the various phenomena. Accordingly, I changed my approach and my goals. Rather than trying to find evidence or truth, I began to look for things that were truly new and innovative in the various paranormal practices.

Unfortunately, I discovered a wasteland of "non-ideas," with only a few rare and thought-provoking exceptions. The work of Mac Tonnies was intriguing, and his reasoned speculation on the possibilities of ancient ruins on Mars was light years ahead of Richard Hoagland's sadly repetitive nonsense about hyper-dimensional physics and Masonic conspiracies.[4] As the world-wide-web developed, more voices emerged, whether through blogging, conversing on discussion boards, or their own videos and podcasts. Some of these voices were interesting because they provided new viewpoints on old cases and well-worn theories, but many of these were, once again, little more than old ideas and old evidence in new 21st century packaging.

---

[3] Mark Pilkington, *Mirage Men: A Journey into Disinformation, Paranoia and UFOs* (Constable, 2010); Greg Bishop, *Project Beta: The Story of Paul Bennewitz, National Security, and the Creation of a Modern UFO Myth* (Gallery Books, 2005).

[4] See Mac Tonnies, *After The Martian Apocalypse: Extraterrestrial Artifacts and the Case for Mars Exploration* (Paraview Pocket Books, 2004).

Remix. Reuse. Recycle.

This is not, you understand, a criticism. As I will lay out in the following chapters, I've come to suspect that the notions of writers like John Keel and George Hansen are more plausible than not. Keel, Hansen, and others have postulated that the phenomena themselves are actively elusive, evading our attempts to understand them. Our theories and thoughts run in circles because, in some cases, that is all they can manage. Like shining a laser pointer in a hall of mirrors, our focus and attention bounces around from aliens to ghosts to hidden civilizations, constantly trying to explain the individual pieces or connect them into a unified field theory of The Weird.

We have not, of course, gotten there yet. Maybe we never will.

But in the meantime, the various memes and thought forms which comprise the paranormal have become inextricably intertwined with various cultural and pop-cultural emanations ranging from novels to the scourge of reality television. The deeper we get into the twenty-first century, the more the lines between investigation, personal experience and entertainment continue to blur. The essays in this book record my attempts to track outbreaks of novelty in the worlds of the paranormal and the larger culture; they also attempt to come to some sort of personal terms with the strange and unusual in our midst.

I am coming at this from the perspective of an historian, but this is not a history of the paranormal or any of the figures involved. As an historian, I am most fascinated by the atemporality of paranormal culture, and the broader popular cultures and subcultures which it inhabits.

The notion of atemporality has been sighted in the culture more and more in the past few years, as digital photography programs and services like Instagram allow users to apply filters to photos that make them look as though they were taken in the 1970s rather than the twenty-first century. Writer Sarah Wanenchak assesses atemporality as follows:

> The intermeshing and interweaving of the physical and digital causes us not only to experience both of those categories differently, but to perceive time itself differently; that for most of us, time is no longer a linear experience (assuming it ever was). Technology changes our remembrance of the past, our experience of the present, and our imagination of the future by blurring the lines between the three categories, and introducing different forms of understanding and meaning-making to all three – We remember the future, imagine the present, and experience the past.[5]

This is, I believe, a useful framework both for considering paranormal experiences themselves as well as for understanding the culture surrounding claims of such experiences. This notion of atemporality goes beyond speculating about whether or not flying saucer occupants are time travelers, or whether ghosts are time travelers. Rather, atemporality is a reflection of how we present and observe our surroundings.

The past and the present of the paranormal are linked in myriad ways. Roswell, for example, is the never-ending story, towering over discussions and arguments about the UFO phenomenon like some ancient monolith; an

---

[5] Sarah Wanenchak, "The Atemporality of 'Ruin Porn': The Carcass & the Ghost," *The Society Pages*, 16 May 2012, http://goo.gl/PqH89l.

overexposed Stonehenge casting a perpetual shadow over whatever new ideas about alien life emerge. Ghosts, spirits and haunting are atemporality in a barely tangible form – the past, present, and perhaps even the future, overlapping in strange and sometimes unexpected ways.

This book is a loosely connected set of essays which explores and reflects upon a lifetime in the shadow of the paranormal and a present in which I am coming to grips with the increasingly intrusive (in a good way) phenomena of atemporality. This book is not necessarily scholarly, although I trust it will not be frivolous, and, while it is not anything near an autobiography, my life since childhood has been intertwined with stories and myths of The Weird and frightening. Not surprisingly, my life has also been suffused with other non-rational phenomenon, particularly Christianity. Inevitably, my own journey colors my perceptions of the world around me, including the paranormal.

I think of my intellectual life as being like a Venn diagram. Circles representing my work in history, my interest in the culture and folklore of the paranormal, and my fairly orthodox Christian beliefs, overlap in a bizarre common ground where they all get blended together in a speculative stew of semi-confusion. The essays in this book are my attempt to make a meal of that stew and, hopefully, clarify my own thinking. Through doing so, I hope that others will find a path to clarification of their own thoughts and notions.

The world of the paranormal is full of convergence between present and past. Stories continue to be worked over, unfolded, refolded and re-purposed. Occasionally they escape the recursive corral of the paranormal subculture and penetrate the wider popular culture, changing to fit the formats, plots, and needs of various genres. Other ideas remain confined to the anomalous realms, known about by devotees of The Weird but not by the man or woman on "the street." These more obscure ideas shift and morph as well, changing in some respects to adapt to the times, yet also remaining oddly timeless. In the following pages, one of the things I will delve into is this timelessness – the continuing overlap between the paranormal past and the paranormal present.

Of course, musings on atemporality will only take us so far. The stories that turn up again and again resonate deeply with us and with the culture at large. The paranormal sub-culture and the broader monoculture exist side by side, occasionally blending or overlapping. At those intersection points iterations of these stories burst out, adding new spark to the old, tired tales. Along with atemporality, I will be exploring some of the stories and figures I believe have contributed to the longevity of this subject.

For the past two decades I've been on an exciting intellectual journey which has taken me from Roswell and MJ-12 to Ashtar and Exopolitics, with a bit of Gray Barker and the Mothman thrown in for good measure. These stories are no doubt familiar to many readers, and I am not as interested in retelling them as I am in navigating the twists and turns in the overarching narrative to see where and how it intersects with the broader culture. This is a fascinating journey, but it's also one that I make at a certain distance and remove. That, again, is the historian part of me talking. Just as I cannot literally go back in time and evaluate historical events for myself, I cannot go back to Roswell and 1947 and figure out "the truth."

Another factor in this series of explorations and attempted explanations is to work out and express what I actually think of these topics. While working on my purely academic book, *Extraterrestrials and the American Zeitgeist*, friends and colleagues would often ask me what my opinion was of the stories I explored and presented. As an historian, I made a conscious effort to *not* think about Contactees (or any other paranormal topic) in terms of forming an opinion about their veracity or their deeper meaning. That's a dangerous direction in which to go for an academic, and despite whatever personal fascination I had with their individual stories, I had to keep myself somewhat aloof. This book is a welcome opportunity for me to explore the culture of the paranormal from a personal perspective rather than just an academic one. Still, the personal perspective takes place at a bit of a remove. I'm not in the trenches interviewing witnesses, or standing in a field staring at the night sky. Neither am I part of the paranormal subculture. I don't frequent forums; I've never called *Coast to Coast AM*; apart from one book review in 2005, I've never written for *UFO Magazine*. As a matter of objectivity as well as my personality, I cling to my little redoubt of separation and isolation.

There are, of course, some exceptions to this aloofness. In 1996, I "investigated" a real, live crop circle, which was the closest I ever got to something that might be considered "paranormal," at least to my knowledge. At the time, my friend and I were just having a laugh at the expense of other people who were there because they were both more earnest and more paranoid than we were. Fifteen years later, however, I look at the situation differently. There is personal atemporality at work as well, as I consider how this bizarre little episode – a few hours out of the decades of my life – has kept surfacing in conversations, memory and even writings like this. I've been to a supposedly haunted cemetery and while I didn't see a ghost, the entire experience was undeniably *freaky*. Even my rule against on-line forum participation has an

Aaron John Gulyas

astoundingly weird exception, which plunged me briefly into a web of deceit, paranoia, and madness. As I will relate, every personal foray into the phenomena has ended badly, weirdly, or served to illustrate my own obnoxious immaturity.

Therefore, like the paranormal itself, the stories and explorations in this book blur lines between scholarship and speculation, between personal and universal. Like paranormal events and the paranoid thoughts that often accompany them, writing and thinking about these topics often gets twisted and confused. In the essays that follow, I have attempted to impose an order that does not seek to explain the causes of these myriad phenomena, but rather one that illustrates the effects of our efforts to understand and share them.

There is also an unfortunate and somewhat bizarre overlap between politics, religion and the paranormal which I will explore here as well. Atemporality plays a role in this, as in most other things, as political ideologies and theological obsessions from the past shape perceptions of the present and portend futures that are variously triumphant and desperate. The connections between various strands of political and paranormal thought as well as the links between piety and paranoia tie together diverse topics, often in ways that surprise us.

In the end, I'm not attempting to make sense of the paranormal in its various manifestations; rather, I'm trying to come to some conclusions about my own feelings and experiences. This is an effort to purge the ghosts from my mind and the demons from my thoughts.

Join me.

I took this with the Instagram application on my not-entirely-state-of-the-art mobile phone in Autumn, 2012. One thing that such photos do (and there are, of course, better examples than mine) is free the subject from the context of time and – often – place. This aerial array is temporally located in the present, but the monochrome treatment of the photo that I used gives it a faux-aged appearance. Similarly, the structure puts one in mind of some manner of futuristic surveillance equipment, tracking the chips in our brains and reporting our movements and thoughts to some sinister Big Brother figure. The feelings of atemporality stem from the way certain images convey cultural signifiers. This is, of course, highly personal. Not everyone who looks at this photograph would see it as a fictionalized relic of a future past.

Chapter One
GHOSTS

I work in Flint, Michigan, not far from the downtown area, and occasionally I set out to explore the city.

And I see the ghosts.

Not ghosts in the paranormal, "haunted house" sense. Rather, ghosts and hauntings in the sense meant by Jacques Derrida. In his 1993 book *Specters of Marx*, he discussed the notion that Marxist ideas would haunt the world long after the philosophy's "moment" had passed.[6] Today, the term "hauntology" connotes a more general sense of atemporality – past and present overlapping in art, music, and architecture. A great example is the music of Belbury Poly, which sounds like nothing if not the lost soundtrack to every 1970s *Doctor Who* episode.[7]

Writers and futurists like Warren Ellis and James Bridle, along with designers such as Russell Davies, have identified atemporality with the emerging digital culture in cities. On this point, writing on the *Guardian* website in June 2011, Andrew Gallix discussed the connection between hauntology, cities and the digital: "Smartphones, for instance, encourage us never to fully commit to the here

---

[6] Jacques Derrida, *Specters of Marx: The State of the Debt, the Work of Mourning & the New International* (Routledge, 1994).

[7] "Belbury Poly on Ploughman's Lunches, Prog Rock and Avoiding Clarkson / Wakeman Territory," *Fact Magazine*, 1 February 2012. http://goo.gl/tfTWDl. See also: "Belbury Poly," *Ghost Box*. http://goo.gl/v028wa.

and now, fostering a ghostly presence-absence."[8]

Despite the presence of smartphones in nearly every hand I see (including my own), I have a difficult time reconciling Flint, Michigan, with the notion of a digital future. Flint is rusting, decaying analogue. That is not, of course, meant as a disparaging comment. The analogue compost of Flint, and other post-industrial rustbelt cities, will, in time, produce little shoots and leaves of the new. Outbreaks of the future, springing up from cracks in the sidewalk, will eventually take over.

We can build a new, shiny, digital world, but the ghosts will always remain. That's the nature of atemporality – history confronting us at every turn. Flint, and other cities like it, do not find themselves in a particular economic condition solely because of current political policies or practices. Rather, the weight of years worth of commerce and culture shapes the present and, to a degree, determines the options from which civic leaders can choose in their attempts to create a brighter future. Regardless of their choices, the scars of poor decision making and sometimes just plain old bad luck will remain.

Likewise, the ghosts will never leave. They will continue to "haunt" the neighborhoods, and linger on the streets. We may see a liquor store in a strip mall. On that site was a residential neighborhood. Dig down, excavate the layers, and find the stables and blacksmiths' forges.

The more you dig, the more likely that you'll find the ghosts. After all, we built our cities on their ethereal bones, as our children will someday build on ours. Someday, *we'll* be the ghosts.

---

[8] Andrew Gallix, "Hauntology: A not-so-new critical manifestation," *The Guardian*, 17 June 2011, http://goo.gl/82yACk.

Occasionally, here and there, I see references to something called archaeoacoustics. Broadly, archaeoacoustics is the study of how humans may have used the acoustic properties of various spaces. A couple of generations ago, however, some archaeologists speculated that we could gain much more direct information from the past, using sound. According to *Wikipedia*:

> An early interpretation of the idea of archaeoacoustics was that it explored acoustic phenomena encoded in ancient artifacts. For instance, the idea that a pot or vase could be 'read' like a gramophone record or phonograph cylinder for messages from the past, sounds encoded into the turning clay as the pot was thrown.[9]

This notion of archaeoacoustics, if legitimate, is an amazing demonstration of atemporality. For historians, this would be a valuable tool for understanding how spaces and objects have been used in the past.

If it is a legitimate phenomenon, and if the techniques to take advantage of it are reliable, it raises interesting questions about other forms of "information energy" which may be present all around us. Could "ghosts" be a similar form of information energy, perhaps more kinetic than acoustic? If flooding areas or objects with certain types of "pink noise" bring forth sounds from the past, we could theoretically flood allegedly haunted spaces with a similar kind of frequency and call forth whatever energies might be present.

We could, in essence, "haunt" the ghosts.

EVP is an iteration of this although, like "reverse

---

[9] "Archaeoacoustics," *Wikipedia*, http://goo.gl/mXe8si.

speech," it is subject to a kind of auditory paradoia. The same phenomena which causes people to pick out and see visual patterns which might not exist (like "faces" on Mars) causes people to find sounds, words, and meanings where none may exist. Regardless, it is an interesting exercise in new applications of technology to studying the past.

For example, imagine the value to historians if we could flood Athenian ruins with the right frequency and discern not just the words, but the voice of Socrates. It is one thing to read the writings of those who participated in the creation of the United States Constitution in 1787, but it would be much more enlightening to listen to their debates and arguments. Could we dose Constitution Hall with the right kind of static and pick the right signals out of the noise?

My point is that for all the spooky, paranormal connotations surrounding the concepts of ghosts and haunting, these are fascinating aspects which contain exciting "real world" possibilities for a wider understanding of the world around us and the world that existed in the past.

So let us think of ghosts as something more pervasive than merely the spirits of the dead. Imagine that what we consider to be "ghosts" are a tangible manifestation of a historical residue; an invisible, non-corporeal version of dried blood – what author Warren Ellis called "the moments where the past can be heard leaking through the walls."[10] Perhaps someday a forensic technician will dust for prints, find DNA, and record background acoustic and visual data from the site of a murder, use computers to recreate the sights and sounds of the killing, and present it

---

[10] Warren Ellis, "A Hauntological Literature," *Warren Ellis*, 11 December 2012, www.warrenellis.com/?p=14540.

all as evidence. If that sounds far-fetched, just remember that a century ago DNA profiling would have sounded similarly magical.

Eruptions of the past into the present are not a new phenomenon. Neither is their occasional ghostly, haunting quality. I have a family photograph that is a good example of this idea of haunting – of history emerging, summoned by cultural or personal desire to commune with the past in some way.

The photograph dates from 1932 and is of my maternal grandmother's family. On the right-hand side of the picture is my great uncle Clarence. What is significant about Clarence appearing in this picture is that he died several years before it was taken, a victim of influenza. He was inserted into the photograph (photo manipulation did not, after all, begin with Photoshop) in order to provide a more complete image of the family in happier times.

Although the image of Clarence is slightly out of proportion to the rest of the family members, as a child I didn't notice anything out of the ordinary about the picture until my mother pointed it out. Once I knew that Clarence had been "photo-shopped" in, the picture (which had always fascinated me – who knew that grandmothers and great uncles could ever possibly have been young?) became a slight obsession for a time, as I studied it intently, trying to pinpoint the joins in the photo and determine the methods used to create the amalgamated image.

My sister always thought it was creepy to have inserted "a dead guy" into a picture, but I always thought it was completely understandable. This family photo was not necessarily meant to be a piece of literal documentary evidence of the Scheumann family in 1932. Rather, it represents a narrative, a story of the family as an ideal. The act of inserting a lost family member into the photograph was an act of summoning a ghost; an attempt to bring forth a means to ameliorate the loss of a loved one. Perhaps it was an effort (conscious or unconscious) to replace one haunting with another, to substitute a lingering sense of loss with a more tangible, accessible, and altogether more comforting memory.

Whatever the reason, the effect is – and there is no other word for it – haunting. Such examples of atemporality are often jarring and strange. Our minds, in many ways, are accustomed to running in linear fashion. When the timeline – be it architectural or personal – is out of order, a shiver runs through us.

But this photograph, regardless of how I might try to fit it into this strange and somewhat pretentious postmodern paradigm of hauntology, is never going to be a fit subject for a traditional ghost hunting television series – although, I must say, a television show that focused on tracking outbreaks of atemporality and features experts on hauntology would be something I would watch constantly. How do we connect the two ideas and phenomena?

One way to think about it would be to consider both types of event to be manifestations of history. Traditional hauntings are unbidden manifestations of tangible history – smells, sounds, temperature changes, hazy images, all pushing through into our present. Unlike architectural, cultural, artistic, or personal expressions of atemporality, traditional hauntings often involve the presence of unwanted, even frightening elements. Atemporal phenomena and "haunted" spaces, which are specifically created or sought out, can be disturbing and disorienting. How much more so are those that appear uninvited?

Perhaps it would be a mistake to attempt to draw some sort of artificial line between "traditional" hauntings and those that we accept as part of our everyday lives. In the end, like most things, we tend to create distinctions without differences. In the case of hauntings and ghosts, the distinction comes down to the context of a particular event or experience. A child's voice emanating from the next room when you know there's no child there; the decaying remains of the industrial landscapes of a bygone era, with its attendant social, economic, and cultural displacements.

Both are ghosts.

Both are examples of the past haunting our present.

I just haven't decided which one should scare me more.

My great uncle Clarence appears in this family photo (back row, second from right), even though he died of influenza several years before it was taken – he was inserted afterwards, an example of atemporality at work. Photo alteration like this, only in reverse, was common practice in the Soviet Union under Stalin, where members of the Communist Party who had fallen from favor (and who had usually been executed) were removed from official photos.

Chapter Two
EXPERIENCES

I have never actually investigated a paranormal event. Nor have I "investigated" a painting or a piece of music. Writers such as Greg Bishop, Paul Kimball, and Mac Tonnies have described paranormal events as being akin to performance art by whatever entities (if any) may be responsible for them. Having no aptitude for science and engaging in logical, reasoned thought only with great difficulty, I've adopted the same attitude, and plunged myself – albeit briefly – into two particular situations that had an effect on how I view others' accounts of paranormal activities.

This is not because I believe I had direct supernatural experiences. Rather, these experiences demonstrated to me how others could come to believe that various encounters were, perhaps, outside the bounds of conventionally understood science and rationality.

The first encounter with what might be reasonably considered an actual paranormal experience occurred in July, 1996. I was at home in Columbia City, Indiana for summer break after my sophomore year at Hanover College. The following account is – shockingly, and a little sadly – accurate, even down to the melodramatic dialogue.

I was, at that time, deeply into the idea of investigating the paranormal. I had even joined an organization to help find opportunities. I was also very bored.

I'd been the head of UFO Investigation Agency Strategic Investigation Team 1310 for quite a while by that time. The UFOIA was an alleged investigatory body I had joined the previous year. As the lead member of SIT 1310, I patiently waited on a call or email requesting me to check out some sinister sighting or anomalous encounter. No calls ever came my way. Despite the fact that I had an authentic identification card, my services were not requested by the head of the organization, a shadowy figure calling himself Randolph B. Warneke. I was getting frustrated. Had I seen one flying saucer? No! Had any Men in Black warned me to keep my mouth shut? No!

So, one Tuesday afternoon after getting home from work, I picked up the *Post & Mail* to see which of my high school classmates had been arrested that particular day. On the front page was a headline that would change my entire day:

CROP CIRCLE IN THORNCREEK TOWNSHIP

I threw down the paper and grabbed the phone. I dialed the number of Doug, a longtime friend and fellow bored college student. Busy. I redialed. Doug picked up before the first ring.

"I just tried to call you. Did you see the paper?" Doug's voice was breathless with excitement.

"I just tried to call *you*. You wanna go check it out?"

"Yeah, give me half an hour."

I quickly slipped on a tweed sport coat, primarily because it was the sort of thing I pictured paranormal investigators wearing. Even in July.

I grabbed my camera and tape recorder, told the folks where I was going, and headed out the door. I climbed into my 1985 Toyota Camry and headed toward town. As I drove, I mused on my situation. It was clear that we had no idea what the circle might look like, how close we would be able to get, or anything else. Within what seemed like mere minutes I was pulling the Camry into Doug's driveway.

The garage door was open and I went in. Doug was there – clad in black pants, black turtleneck and a pale trench coat: obviously what he thought paranormal investigators wore. Even in July.

More shocking, he was holding a strange device. Grey in color, it had a light mounted on it, and a long rod extending from the end, topped with a cork.

"Doug, what *is* that?" I queried.

"It's a paranormal energy detector," he answered with a serious look on his face, making me wonder if his mind had finally gone. "I took an old slide projector, taped a Black & Decker Snake-light under it, and put a metal rod on the end. Pretty cool, huh?"

A fake detection device seemed like just the sort of thing we needed to take with us. With Doug in his trench coat and yours truly in my Sherlock Holmes-ian tweed, we probably looked like a couple of morons – particularly since the temperatures were hovering in the mid-80s.

The circle was north of town, just off Indiana highway 109, deep in the midst of Thorncreek Township. Being unfamiliar with the area, we drove slowly, not wanting to miss it. Within fifteen minutes (about 10 miles outside of town), we saw a number of cars parked near an intersection. I pulled our official alien-hunting vehicle safely off to the side of the road and we embarked on our greatest adventure yet.

There were maybe five other people looking at the circle. It was about two hundred feet from the road, and the field was surrounded by yellow police "caution" tape. Doug and I stared at it wordlessly, trying to comprehend something so beautiful and mysterious. We were cast into an almost spiritual state.

"What should we do?" I asked.

There didn't seem to be a lot to investigate from the road, and if we went into the field with that many witnesses around, we would certainly be detained by the authorities. We liked to think that the county officials would disapprove of our efforts to bring THE TRUTH to light, and we weren't looking for trouble.

"Let's try out the paranormal energy detector," Doug suggested. Without waiting for my answer, he moved off to the ditch next to the field and pointed the PED toward the ground. He walked along slowly, looking through the viewfinder. Suddenly, he began calling off numbers.

"Four-point-seven. Five-point-eight. Are you getting these, Aaron?"

Thinking fast, I switched on the tape recorder and repeated the numbers into the mic.

"Got 'em Doug," I answered. "Keep going!"

I suppressed a smile. If we couldn't get close to the circle, there was no reason we couldn't confound the bystanders. We continued our charade for a few minutes but, aside from curious looks from a few of the other people on site, received no other response.

The sun was starting to set, and people slowly drifted away. We walked up the road, trying to see if there was a way into the field that wouldn't be easily detectable.

"So what do you think it is, Doug?"

"Well, it could be a lot of things," he replied. "Plasma induction technology could have been used to create it, but I won't know until we get to the center. There's trademark blistering of the stalks when that method is used."

I bristled at Doug's use of the passive voice.

"Could have been used by whom? Are we dealing with aliens or an earthbound phenomenon? I know as our projectile design specialist you're looking at the technological aspects of this, but UFOIA HQ wants answers and they want them quickly. SIT 1310 is really on the bubble right now. We could lose our certification if we don't come up with some answers soon!"

Yes, we really had this conversation, with the tape recorder still running (more on that tape later). We strained to keep our voices filled with seriousness, hoping that the bystanders would engage with us in some way. Doug and I, for whatever reason, seemed to lapse into a kind of Walter Mitty-like double-act on occasion (and still do, nearly two decades later). None of the people standing around talked to us, asked us questions, or even asked to see my official UFOIA Investigator's ID card (which was fortuitous, because I had, in fact, forgotten to bring the card with me).

We stepped into the ditch, trying to decide whether or not we should enter the wheat field, when we heard a faint buzzing sound. Looking down the road, we saw a four-wheel ATV coming toward us. The rider was middle-aged, scraggly, wearing camouflage, and smoking a cigarette. Doug and I shared a look that could only be described as "fearful."

"You guys here for the crop circle?" he called as he slowed to a stop.

I bounded up to him.

"Yes! We're investigators for the UFO Information Agency, Strategic Investigation Team 1310. I'd show you my identification, but I've left my wallet at home."

He looked at me with cold, bloodshot eyes. In an instant, Doug was standing there as well.

"Did you watch the news," he asked the mysterious rider. "They say it's fake."

The stranger didn't sound like he agreed. "They say it's fake because someone found a cigarette in the middle of it this morning. You know what?"

"No, we don't," Doug replied, his eyes wide with

wonder and fear. Mostly fear.

"That was my cigarette. I was out here before anyone else saw it and I dropped my cigarette. That means it's not fake."

"Wow," I said, struggling to not point out that someone could have created it *before* he arrived with his cigarette. "That would certainly put a dent in any hoaxing argument. What time were you out here?"

"About four. Maybe earlier. I don't know. I know a lot about this sort of thing."

He stared at Doug and me, as if daring us to contradict him.

"Oh yeah, I've got a stack of magazines at home all about it." He stopped abruptly. "But I shouldn't be telling you guys that, should I? You probably already know all about me."

"Um…" Doug stammered.

"Er…" I added.

"That's what I thought," the man said with a slight nervous laugh.

I thought quickly. "No, I mean, we aren't from the government or anything. Really, we're not even real investigators; we're just a couple of college kids home on break."

"Yeah," Doug interjected. "We're not keeping track of you or anything."

The man started to back away. "Sure. Sure. I bet that's what you tell everyone."

"No, we're really just a couple of guys," I replied. "It's nothing more than that!"

I could see that he didn't believe us. Without saying another word, he turned his ATV around and sped off down the road.

At this point, Doug and I decided that crossing the

yellow police tape and entering the wheat field wasn't the best idea. For one thing, it was trespassing, and doing a stint in the Whitley County lockup didn't appeal to us. For another, it was a really long walk out to where the circle was located and we were already dripping with sweat from our poor "in character" clothing choices. We started walking back to the car when we noticed a rickety van heading toward us in the twilight.

The van stopped and two figures got out. One was a generally clean-cut looking fellow. His companion appeared to be some sort of aging hippy, right down to her lavender-tinted John Lennon glasses.

"Hello!" she called, jogging toward us. "Have you been into the center yet?"

"Um, no, we haven't," answered Doug as he walked towards them.

"What's that?" the man asked, pointing to the PED.

"Well, it's a paranormal energy detector," Doug replied, looking nervously in my direction for confirmation.

The woman turned to me.

"I took a course on crop circles at the local campus of Indiana and Purdue Universities," she said. "The energy is concentrated in the center of the circle."

"Ah… well, that would make sense," I said, not knowing what else I should say. I wanted to ask why IPFW was offering courses on crop circles, but didn't want to seem like a square, not "hip" to the "scene."

"If you like," she continued, "we could take your device into the circle with us to get the readings you need."

If they went into that circle with the PED, the jig would be up. We stammered for a few moments, trying to come up with a reason why they shouldn't do this tremendous favor for us. I couldn't think of anything to say, so luckily Doug spoke up.

"Thanks, but I don't think that's a good idea. The PED is just a prototype. We just got the plans from UFOIA headquarters this morning. I'm not even sure it really works."

"Yeah," I added. "Knowing the shoddy material and equipment they usually send us, it probably doesn't work at all." I smiled in what I hoped was a winning manner. "Thanks for the offer, though."

We then said goodbye to them and started back toward the car. Like most investigators of the unknown, we were left with more questions than answers. Where did the circle come from? Was it made by human hands, or by something or someone beyond our world? Perhaps whatever caused it is part of our planet, some kind of force that we hadn't yet figured out how to harness. There was no way to tell, with our bumbling interviews and misadventures with imaginary paranormal energy detectors.

"Any ideas?" I asked.

"None whatsoever," Doug answered. "I don't know why things like this happen?"

"What do you mean? The circle, or me forgetting my wallet, or the hippies, or what?"

Doug's face fell. "No, things like us seeing the story in the paper at the same time, the colliding phone calls, the fact that neither of us had anything to do tonight, all of it."

"Well, to be fair," I countered, "we almost never have anything to do. But I see what you mean. This all feels a little too contrived to be coincidence. Yet, if it's *not* a coincidence, then who's behind it?"

"Exactly!"

"I have a feeling the answer will come in time," I said. "The real question is, are we *ready* for the answer?"

We drove back toward town, as silent as the field we'd just left.

Fifteen years later, the Whitley County Crop Circle still resonates with me. Part of the reason is that I had so much darn fun messing with earnest weirdoes and suspicious, grizzled paranoiacs. Another reason is the set of coincidences that, when taken as a whole, just seems to be slightly less than probable.

First, there was the tape. The recorder into which I repeated those "paranormal energy readings" stayed running in my jacket pocket, unseen by the people we encountered. It was, honestly, pretty funny. I played the tape for others one time, a few weeks later. Among those listening was my future wife. Five years later when we re-met at a party, she remembered that tape vividly. I'm not saying we got married because she enjoyed the crop circle tape, but it didn't hurt.

The tape disappeared after that one airing. I'm not arguing that the government broke into my house and confiscated it (to keep me from THE TRUTH, of course), but I don't think I simply misplaced it. Maybe it just didn't need to exist past that first listen. Yes, I know that makes no sense. I'm not sure it has to.

The UFOIA certainly did exist, and I was the lead investigator for Strategic Investigation Team 1310. They no longer do, though. I can find no trace of them on the internet, aside from a "UFO Directory" listing linking their old, now vanished AOL homestead website. The UFOIA provided a useful fiction for Doug and I to look at the crop circle, which led to the tape, which helped lead to my current happy life. Like the tape, the UFOIA vanished when it was no longer needed.

I certainly didn't imagine the crop circle. Local newspapers reported it, and an experienced crop circle investigator named Roger Sugden looked into it. I ran into Sugden a few years ago at the Indiana MUFON state meeting. He told me, vaguely, that there were some "very unusual" circumstances to the Whitley County circle, although he wouldn't elaborate. He promised to send me a copy of the report, which he never did.[11]

The upshot to this is that the entire experience was a bit strange. Any conclusions I have attempted to draw have been vague and unsatisfying. I have been running it over and over in my head since it happened. Like just about every "paranormal" phenomenon, I think these things have meaning that is more significant on an individual level than on a universal, scientific one. The experience was meaningful for me and my life. The fact that the circle itself was in all likelihood a hoax doesn't change that. One of the greatest lessons I learned from this experience is the effect that the presence of this alleged circle had on those who witnessed it. In the people on that rural road I saw fear, wonder, and confusion. In myself and Doug, I recognize mischief and, to a degree that I'm somewhat ashamed of now, a glee in prodding the credulous people we met. For all my sense of superiority in not *really* believing in any mysterious or paranormal origins of the crop circle, I was out there in the road like the rest of them. What made me any better than they were?

Regardless of what the origins of these phenomena may be – whether prosaic or inexplicable – I am increasingly convinced that one of the roles that they play, in their frustrating "tricksterish" way, is to humble us. This constellation of events and ideas torments us by being, seemingly, forever out of reach of our powers of observational and empirical investigation. Part of this, I

---

[11] Sugden is a founder of Independent Crop Circles Researchers' Association. See: "ICCRA Member Profile: Roger Sugden," *ICCRA*. http://goo.gl/HlDkMO.

believe, is to put us in our place – to show us that not everything in our world is susceptible to logic and reason.

The second experience took place in 1999 or 2000 near Bloomington, Indiana. I was visiting my old friend Andy Gage and his girlfriend Shelly (they have since married). Andy and Shelly have, for a long time, been actively engaged in examining the question of haunted spaces. To be honest, at the time, I thought that ghosts and haunting ranked somewhere below reliable police psychics and the lost continent of Mu on the probability scale. Ufology, I contended, was where "it" was at. What "it" was, I had not yet concluded (still haven't, actually). Of course, I was still stuck in the conventional mode of thinking of "ghosts" as the spirits of dead folk who had unfinished business here in this mortal realm and not in the more philosophical way I do now ("philosophical" being a synonym for "weird" in this instance).

So that was, briefly, my attitude toward ghosts. Disdainful, skeptical. Andy and Shelly, clearly wishing me some kind of psychological harm, suggested paying a visit to historic and allegedly haunted Stepp Cemetery, located just off US 37 on some back road in the midst of the Morgan-Monroe State Forest. I assented, thinking it would be fun. To be honest, it *was* fun, but only in retrospect. At the time, however, I would have been hard pressed to describe the experience as anything less than unnerving.

Regardless of whether or not Stepp Cemetery is haunted, it has an interesting history. According to Troy Taylor, author of *Beyond the Grave: The History of America's Most Haunted Cemeteries*:

> No one really seems to know when the burial ground was started, or by who. Forest rangers will tell visitors that some area families founded it, but local rumors state that a now defunct

religious cult called the "Crabbites" may have had some connection to it. Apparently, this peculiar sect conducted services that included snake handling, speaking in tongues and sex orgies. Local lore has it that a deputy from the area once stated that he had been called to the cemetery late one night to break up a particularly bizarre Crabbite ritual. The story says that he had to use a bullwhip to settle things down![12]

There are a number of potential spirits that one might encounter, generally women or girls. Clearly, there is a long history to the place and, in daylight, it would be a fascinating site to study. But I didn't go in daylight.

After dinner at a Red Lobster during which Andy and Shelly told me some of the many stories of odd occurrences at this cemetery, we hit the road and made our way out there. Stepp Cemetery is located at the end of a narrow dirt track, so after parking the car just off the highway, we had a bit of a trek. I don't know how many of you reading this have walked down a lonely dirt track towards a cemetery in the dark, but I'm not sure I'd recommend it. As we got closer and closer to the actual cemetery, I felt anxiety building and the dark got deeper. We got to the old, worn tombstones, stood around for a while, talked, and failed to spot anything we could reliably consider a ghost.

As we turned to walk back down that narrow dirt track to our car the night started to close in a bit more. The trees seemed to be extending their branches over the trail and something – a ghost, or was it just foliage – brushed against my face. I must not have been the only one of us

[12] Troy Taylor, "Strange Legends of Stepp Cemetery," *Prairie Ghosts*, 1998. http://goo.gl/ngwhqP.

experiencing this because, simultaneously, we all decided that running was a better way to get back to the car than walking.

Although none of us had actually seen anything ghostly or paranormal, I felt as if something that was literally "out of the ordinary" had happened. I was gripped by an anxiety and fear that I had not experienced up to that point. As a result I was psychologically taken to a state of mind I had not previously encountered. This is all, of course, explainable through science and reason. But that does not make the feelings themselves any more comforting. If someone had said to me, "calm down, all of this is just in your head," I probably would have just hit him and kept running. Irrational fear does that sort of thing to a person.

All of this is just in your head.

I can think of few things more frightening than a phenomenon that is intangible and unknowable to everyone except the one who is experiencing it. Could this array of phenomena that masquerades as ghosts, lights in the sky, or anything else be able to penetrate our actual psyche? It certainly felt that way a dozen years ago when I was running down that lane in southern Indiana. What we describe as hauntings could be similar to a kind of fugue state or, less scientifically, a vision. When multiple people experience a haunting, it puts me in mind of theories about the collective unconscious. Strange noises, odd chills, and mysterious echoes might, under some circumstances, be in *all* of our heads.

A final frightening and disturbing experience had nothing to do with the supernatural, at least as far as any personal encounters of mine were concerned. Rather, I discovered some examples of the extreme levels of paranoia and irrationality prevalent at the intersection of politics, religion, and the paranormal.

One preliminary note about this story is in order. I am going to do my best to convey these events using pseudonyms for the people involved. The reason is that the key players in this sordid little tale are still active in these fields. Since Google can now, very efficiently, search within the text of books, I would very much like to stay as far off of these peoples' radar as possible. As you read the following account, I hope you will understand my decision.

It was 2005, and I was once again bored. Teaching history and philosophy part time at a small, rural community college in Illinois was professionally fulfilling, but the part-time nature meant I had a lot of spare time on my hands. As I was wont to do, I spent a good deal of that spare time poking around the more bizarre corners of the Internet, and I came across a website that claimed to have information (gleaned from the website owner's "investigative journalism") about an insidious plot to round up "right thinking" Americans, which is to say those who opposed the coming New World Order, and imprison them in Nazi-style concentration and death camps.

What fascinated me was that the "evidence" for this story was, for the most part, recycled information from the height of the 1990s patriot-movement paranoia (a subject I will explore in a bit more detail in the later chapter dealing with the tale of William Cooper). I took it upon myself to place a comment on the website's message board, pointing out the fact that the "investigation" on the site was regurgitated, and called into question the journalistic credentials of the owner (whom I will call "Jimmy").

Jimmy, it turned out, had a history with some of the visitors to the site. "Frank" and his wife had given Jimmy a place to stay when he was down on his luck, and they felt they had been taken advantage of. Another commenter on the site – call her "Tracy" – claimed to have evidence that

Jimmy was a government agent, a provocateur whose job was to spread disinformation. Tracy seemed to be a bit nuts, but this was all very entertaining to me, so I made a fateful decision.

I set up my own message board, ostensibly dedicated to serving as a watchdog for Jimmy and his fellows, spreading their iffy information. In truth, I thought it would be an interesting laboratory for examining the attitudes of these paranoiacs, yammering about this, that, or the other government conspiracy. The figures on this message board were all convinced of the reality of the coming tribulation, as described in John's *Revelation*. This was a period in which Christians would be hideously persecuted by a "one world government," or the Catholic Church, or the American government, or some hideous combination of all of them. Aliens were likely real, but were just as likely demons in disguise.

As I continued to track the connections between these different ideas, I saw links between what the people on my message board discussed and the theories of Bill Cooper, and strong overtones of the para-evangelical fringe. I exalted in these connections. I had a forum in which I could prod these discussion board members to talk about the strange stuff I wanted to learn about, sharing their theories, ideas, and fears. For a few golden weeks, I was having a great time. I even played a little practical joke on Tracy, in which I posed as an alien/demon hybrid and declared her our mortal enemy.

This is where it all started to fall apart. Tracy, it turns out, wasn't just a bit nuts; she was insane.

I had been getting some emails from Frank. He'd discovered that Tracy was, in fact, the person behind about a half dozen different personalities on my little message board. In addition, she'd been emailing several people telling them that she'd deciphered my screen-name. It was, she claimed, mentioned in the "Bible Codes" and proved that I was, in fact, the spawn of Satan and a government agent. This was all very amusing until Tracy went beyond Bible Codes and did some digging around on the internet, namely IP addresses and the like.

She sent me an email in which she told me my real name, where I lived, and where I worked. She rambled on about being on a mission from God to eliminate evil from the world. Evil like me.

At this point, I had the distinctly unpleasant experience of telling my wife what I'd been up to in my spare time. She was irritated with me, and wondered if we were in any actual danger. I didn't think so, but I still made an effort to cut off all contact to anyone with whom I'd been involved in this whole sordid little adventure. I had idle daydreams of needing to defend my home with *Die Hard* style shenanigans, along with more sedate and useful investigations into the local Sherriff's department's phone number.

It all died down after a while. I have mostly stayed out of those particular corners of the Internet ever since, peeking in only occasionally to see if the key figures in the story were still insane (they were). I was more bewildered by these paranoid Internet people than I was by the hippie lady at the crop circle. I was more terrified of my interactions with them than I was when I was dashing down that dirt track in Monroe County, Indiana. I learned in a frighteningly first-hand way that the ideas I was content to consider as a fun thought-experiment were life and death "truths" to others.

The lesson, like that of my crop circle lark, was that while the paranormal and the paranoid may be dealt with in a light-hearted manner, it is best not to mock the people or the ideas. Like my encounter with the "spirits" of Stepp Cemetery, I also learned that our perceptions play a crucial role in shaping the reality of the paranormal. The weight of their knowledge of what they saw as the collusion between the American government and the demonic forces masquerading as extraterrestrials warped Tracy's perceptions of the world around her. Everyone and everything bent to her paranoid vision of reality. For a brief period, I was part of that bizarre web of connections, shapes, and ideas that made up her twisted, frightened world.

I know now how real these intangibles can be. All three of these experiences have encouraged me to examine the paranormal and paranoid alike at a healthy remove. Scholarly detachment is not merely an affectation or a job requirement. It is a defense mechanism, protecting me from the insanity of the paranoid as well as the things in the shadows hat *make* them so paranoid.

Deep down, I'm a bit worried that there's something out there I should fear; something that would more than justify the paranoia of the Internet fringe. I'm perfectly happy to ignore that potential truth and stay at the edge of these stories. If we continue along with the idea of the paranormal being – to a degree – sentient, then I'm fine with staying away from its grasp.

Because I think it may feed on us. On our fear, and our paranoia. And I do not intend to provide more than a modest snack.

UFOIA International
Name: *Aaron J.*
Height: *6'1"* Weight: *170* Eyes: *Blue*
Hair: *Brown* SIT No: *1310*

(Signature of Investigator)
This is to certify that
The above Named Person
is an authorized investigator for
UFOIA International.

Randolph B Warneke Director of
Operations UFOIA International

My UFOIA International investigator's card, circa 1996.

CHAPTER THREE

BARKER & MOSELEY: BUILDING WORLDS

I just finished watching *Shades of Gray*, a documentary about the late Gray Barker, a UFO researcher in the 1950s through until his death in 1984.[13] The film is very well done, but I would have liked to have seen the filmmakers address a different take on the hoaxing, misrepresentation of stories, and collusion with various fakers and frauds in which Gray undeniably took part. The film discussed Barker's sense of humor about the subject, but I think there's a case to be made for Barker's hoaxing actually being a form of performance art.

On my trip to the Gray Barker Archives in Clarksburg, West Virginia, I learned a bit about Barker's personal life – particularly about how his activities and sexuality didn't fit very well with small-town West Virginia in the 1950s.[14] I think, perhaps, that the Saucer exploits could have been a kind of pressure release valve for Barker that enabled him to create a world where his outsider status worked to his advantage.

In February, 2012, religious studies scholar David

---

[13] *Shades of Gray*, Dir. Bob Wilkinson, Seminal Films, 2008, http://goo.gl/djmhfG.

[14] The Gray Barker UFO Collection is located at the Clarkson-Harrison Public Library in Clarkson, West Virginia. See: http://goo.gl/t2khVy.

Halperin wrote of Barker:

> The Men in Black, with their hush-up threats and their terror, hovered over Gray Barker each day of his grownup life. That was what gave *They Knew Too Much About Flying Saucers* its tremendous emotional authenticity, calling out to a boy obliged to bear a different secret.[15]

Barker's status as a Myth Maker, creating (or at the very least embellishing and shaping) stories of the Men In Black, reflected the fear he must have felt as a gay man living in 1950s West Virginia. I think, however, that his myth making goes even further than that.

One aspect of Barker's life that I think goes under-examined is his role as a publisher, distributor, and promoter of all manner of Saucer and new age-related materials. His work was about far more than the Men in Black, the Albert K. Bender story, and the International Flying Saucer Bureau.[16] For a generation, Barker was a major source for books, magazines, and pamphlets on The Weird. I believe that this, as much has the Men in Black

---

[15] David Halperin, "Gray Barker, the Men in Black, and North Carolina Amendment One," *The Revealer*, 13 February 2012, http://goo.gl/QHXWFv.

[16] Albert K. Bender was the organizer of the International Flying Saucer Bureau, an American flying saucer club in the 1950s. He claimed to have discovered important data on the origin of UFOs but was allegedly silenced in 1953 by the visit of three mysterious men dressed in black. Three years later this story was recounted by Barker in *They Knew Too Much about Flying Saucers*. The book firmly established the Men in Black (aka MIB) in UFO mythology. In 1962 Bender published his own book, *Flying Saucers and the Three Men* (Saucerian Books, 1963).

aspects of his life that Halperin describes, speak to his embracing of an outsider status far removed from his own particular time and place.

This is particularly true of the Contactees. Barker did a masterful job of promoting them without explicitly endorsing them because he recognized that their stories were interesting, even if they were not true in the literal sense. His editing of these works, such as Bender's *Flying Saucers and the Three Men*, demonstrated a particular viewpoint. He was not just a myth maker, he was a world builder, helping to establish the parameters of a new and exciting collective reality.

The people behind the Gray Barker project at West Virginia University's Center for Literary Computing put it this way:

> Gray Barker's work is an act of literary self-creation. If the postmodern novel troubled the notion of authorship, of intertextual relations, and of the margins between text and context, then the Gray Barker archive is the most extensive, successful, and aporetic postmodern novel ever written.[17]

While they may be overstating it a bit, there is no doubt that Barker's collected output represents something truly significant.

Barker died when I was a child, long before I knew about flying saucers in any detail. The feeling I have when I read his words (and the words of that entire generation of "saucer people") is a nostalgia for something I never experienced. This is due in part to the drab and nihilistic

---

[17] "Gray Barker Project Description," *The Gray Barker Project*, West Virginia University, http://goo.gl/awJ2H5.

world of ufology which my generation inherited in the 1990s, when paranoia replaced whimsy and by-the-numbers dogmatism replaced imaginative blue-sky theorizing. It is also due, however, to the pure, unadulterated fun that can be found in Barker's writings. *They Knew Too Much About Flying Saucers* is one of the few saucer books I can read over and over again.[18]

I think this aspect of unadulterated fun is why I keep coming back to Barker as a sort of touchstone of paranormal and Saucerlogical thought. I respect the work of others, especially theoreticians such as Jacques Vallee, but no one had the sense of art and passion that Barker did. It was almost as if he was subliminally encouraging himself to transcend the limitations of the fast-buck huckster and hoaxer, which was how many people viewed him. Unlike most of his contemporaries, he had a raw and natural gift for making The Weird wonderful, and he embraced it.

Thinking about my intellectual Venn diagram, Gray Barker's work sits right at the intersection of "weird" and "history," occupying a space that always satisfies both interests. Unlike other authors I enjoy, Barker is a bit seasonal. *They Knew Too Much About Flying Saucers* is an "autumn" book for me, and I usually re-read it annually. The decay of the trees and grass conjures feelings of, and affinity for, The Weird. Sometimes my thoughts about these topics drift outside the lines of my personal Venn diagram of interests and intellectual curiosity and venture into the squishier and much idiosyncratic realm of "feeling."

In much the same way as music or scents trigger

---

[18] Gray Barker, *They Knew Too Much About Flying Saucers* (University Books, Inc., 1956). Available on-line at: http://goo.gl/hVaSYZ.

memories, reading *They Knew Too Much About Flying Saucers* evokes some strong memories for me. I remember that autumn over a decade ago when I first read the book as being a transitional time for me – looming work, life, and school issues seemed much more threatening and critical at the time than they do in retrospect. For whatever reasons – real or imagined – I was extraordinarily stressed. Gray Barker's engagingly told story of Albert Bender and the three Men in Black transported me to a time and place when the flying saucer tales with which I was rapidly becoming bored were fresh and new again. The difference between reading Gray Barker's words and slogging through the innumerable UFO-related books I had acquired over the years reminded me of the gulf between reading a poorly-written history textbook and reading the words of Thomas Paine or Abraham Lincoln. The layer of noise, speculation, and assumption I had always found in what I considered the "secondary sources" of ufology was gone. In its place was the fantastical raw material of the myth. Missing were the conspiracy angles that had become so wearisome: Roswell, abductions, MJ-12. Barker's book, written two decades before I was born, was fresher, more vital, and more engaging than the current material available.

Gray Barker's work opened my eyes to how enjoyable the old stories of the 1950s could be. These days, my battered copy of *They Knew Too Much About Flying Saucers* is supplemented with *The Silver Bridge*, Barker's account of the Mothman incidents (an account which captures the mood and character of the region much better than John Keel's more well-known work).[19] Occasionally, I'll dip into some old issues of *The Saucerian*, Barker's seminal saucer 'zine. My devotion to Barker's oeuvre lies not in some great

---

[19] Gray Barker, *The Silver Bridge* (Saucerian Books, 1970).

revelation about the truth of the space beings, because I know that it's not going to be in there. For me, the key to enjoying Barker's work is to consider it an act of art rather than pure reportage or journalism.

Writing, promoting, and producing are just as much forms of performance art as music or dance. I cannot hope to psychoanalyze Gray Barker, but I think David Halperin's view is as close to truth as we may be able to get. As an outsider, with regard to his sexuality if not his interest in flying saucers, Barker created art which served as a distraction or deflection. As Halperin noted, this brought an authenticity to Barker's words which is often absent from even the most well-told eyewitness accounts of paranormal events. Perhaps no other writer connected with the paranormal has done such an effective job of generating an emotional response in me as a reader. The only one who comes close is Whitley Strieber. It's probably not a coincidence that both of these writers blur the line between creating straightforward reports of strange events and conveying personal aspects using techniques that rarely appear in these sorts of books.

In conversations with others who are interested in the paranormal in a vague, general way, even the existence of Gray Barker is largely unknown. The concept of the Men in Black, of course, is well known due to the film series, but the progenitor of the idea is long forgotten. The world of hobbiest 'zines, Contactees, and the Long John Nebel radio show eventually gave way to abductions, conspiracy theories, UFO *Magazine* and Art Bell. Even before his death, Gray Barker's time was over, because the ufological world had supposedly "grown up."

In some ways, I think my fascination with Barker's life and work is a reflection of my occasional desire to have been born in some other time than the one I was. "New" does not always mean better, and I think this is especially true in the field of flying saucers, and the paranormal more generally. When reading Gray Barker, or books by various classic Contactees, I'm undeniably nostalgic for a time I never personally experienced.

Like Gray Barker, his friend James W. Moseley was a somewhat under-heralded figure in the history of ufology. While he was well known to those who study the history of the UFO/Flying Saucer field, he was not as well known outside of that very small group as he should have been. The UFO/Flying Saucer field often suffers from a selective memory, where modern theories, stories, and conjecture constantly call back to Roswell, the 1952 Washington, D.C. "invasion," and other well-worn tales. But the leading figures of times past are often less eager to discuss the people whose work tended to undermine those sacred cows of the UFO myth.

Moseley, who was active in the flying saucer world from the early 1950s until his death in late 2012, was only marginally a UFO/flying saucer investigator. His significance lay in his role as a chronicler of an ever changing scene and the oftentimes strange personalities who inhabited it. His newsletter, published under various names over the decades, but most recently as *Saucer Smear*, offered theories, news, and rumors, but never answers. It was not glossy like *UFO Magazine*, but it was much more informative to students of the field in terms of its history and its development.[20]

Moseley often described himself as ufology's "court jester," but I think that term is an inadequately self-

---

[20] For a heartfelt remembrance of Moseley, see Loren Coleman, "Saucer Smear's James W. Moseley Dies," *Twilight Language*, 18 November 2012. http://goo.gl/Bcbw9N.

deprecating description of a man who was connected, in some way, with nearly every significant figure in the field for almost seven decades. In his autobiography *Shockingly Close to the Truth* (co-authored with the late Karl Pflock), Moseley summed up how he perceived his role in the saucer scene:

> I've long since given up taking the trouble to research UFO events in great depth... as I do have some original thoughts on various ufological topics, the only reasonable role for me in The Field is that of court jester, chiding and poking fun at Serious and Semi-Serious Ufologists and other Leading Lights in such a way that they're not moved to cut me off completely – but may be moved to rethink their various notions and nostrums.[21]

Greg Bishop described him as the "Hunter Thompson of ufology," and I think that term fits him a bit better. Moseley was an integral part in the creation of a subset of UFO thinkers and writers who were interested in the saucer phenomenon but had not been fooled into thinking that it could be easily explained. Unlike some more "serious" commentators, Moseley found the personalities in the flying saucer field as fascinating (if not more fascinating) as the topic of UFOs itself, and philosophical speculation more enticing than cataloging odd lights in the sky.

Barker and Moseley shaped the world of flying saucers and, by extension, the culture at large. It's sometimes difficult to see, half a century on, how central these two men were, but without Barker there would be no tales of

---

[21] James Moseley and Karl T. Pflock. *Shockingly Close to the Truth! Confessions of a Grave-Robbing Ufologist* (Prometheus, 2002).

the ominous Men in Black, less paranoia, perhaps fewer manifestations of stories that describe a shadowy cabal seeking to silence truth-seekers. Think, for a moment, how much of the UFO/Alien/Paranormal milieu is informed by this conspiratorial narrative.

Without Moseley and his "Straith letter," it may have taken longer for a thorough debunking of George Adamski's Contactee stories to appear.[22] Imagine a ufological world where Adamski and his imitators had taken hold as the dominant meme with ufology, relegating the hard-core "scientific" and investigatory organizations like APRO and NICAP into the netherworld of public consciousness to which the Contactees have been banished instead.

It's difficult to imagine. I don't really even want to try, because I find the world they created so much more interesting.

I'd write more, but I think I'm going to go re-read some Gray Barker; even if it's not September, I can still hear his unique voice calling to me, across the void.

---

[22] In 1957, Barker acquired some blank U.S. Governmental letterhead stationery and envelopes from a friend. Moseley and Barker then wrote seven letters, each using this official letterhead. Moseley sent one of the letters to Adamski, signed by the fictional "R.E. Straith," a representative of the non-existent "Cultural Exchange Committee" of the U.S. State Department. "Straith" wrote that the U.S. Government knew that Adamski had actually spoken to extraterrestrials in a California desert in 1952, and that a group of highly placed government officials planned on public corroboration of Adamski's story. Adamski publicized the letter's contents as factual, and when it was revealed to be a hoax he was discredited.

CHAPTER FOUR
SPACE DEMONS !

After reading Nick Redfern's 2010 book *Final Events*, I felt compelled to consider, perhaps against my better judgment, the increasingly troubling connections between paranormal theory and the various forms of Christianity extant in the United States today.[23] Redfern's book tells the story of the Collins Elite, a shadowy group of government insiders who are convinced that alleged space visitors are demonic forces unleashed as a result of occult activities carried out by the likes of rocket engineer and occultist Jack Parsons.[24] This perspective tracks with a resurgence in millennial fundamentalist Christianity. The book is worth reading if for nothing else than the tales of the satisfyingly

---

[23] Nick Redfern, *Final Events* (Anomalist Books, 2010).

[24] John Whiteside Parsons, better known as Jack Parsons, was an American rocket propulsion researcher at the California Institute of Technology and a pioneer in solid rocket fuel research and development. He was one of the principal founders of the Jet Propulsion Laboratory and the Aerojet Engineering Corporation. Parsons was also well known for his interest in the occult and the work of British author and occultist Aleister Crowley. See Colin Bennett, "John Whiteside Parsons," *Fortean Times*, March 2000. Available on-line at: http://goo.gl/JHxGVA. Also, George Pendle, *Strange Angel: The Otherworldly Life of Rocket Scientist John Whiteside Parsons* (Harcourt, Inc., 2006).

creepy figures that Redfern met on his weird journey.

Final Events rekindled my thoughts on the intersection of Christianity and the paranormal, especially the phenomena of flying saucers and extraterrestrial contact and "abductions." Fundamentalist Christianity seems to have gone through some convulsions in the past couple decades. The dispensationalism of the 19th century has been expanded upon, leading to such notions as literal millennialism, a detailed eschatological timeline involving raptures of pre-tribulation, mid-tribulation, or post-tribulation varieties.

Additionally, a political cognate to these religious notions is "dominionism," a concept which links the triumph of Christianity (or at least a nominally Christian set of behavioral and cultural norms) to the dominance of the United States. The tangible element of this can be seen in the connection between fundamentalist thought and American foreign policy, particularly some of the more vehemently pro-Israel/anti-Palestinian movements that can be found in the United States today.

Although I'm a Christian, coming from a Lutheran background, much of the fundamentalist thought floating around our modern cultural landscape baffles me. Personally, I find the institutional blending of faith and politics, and the blithe manner in which some of the more extreme proponents of this relationship toss around the word "theocracy" as though it's not *that* bad of a thing, to be very dangerous. It's fascinating, however, to examine the overlap between some aspects of fundamentalist thought, dominionist political philosophies, and the paranormal. Personalities such as author and radio host Russ Dizdar have made names for themselves by connecting extraterrestrial contact with the familiar tropes of demonic possession or visitation.[25]

As I finished my reading of *Final Events*, I sat in my office, doodling in a notebook, jotting down some thoughts, images, and words inspired by Redfern's book and, as often happens, some of the terms I recorded sparked a memory.

I crossed the office to my dedicated "weird" bookshelf and grabbed a long-forgotten "classic" from Bob Larson: *UFO's and the Alien Agenda*.[26] Larson got his start in the Satanic cult scares of the 1980s, a field plagued by frauds, hucksters, and charlatans such as Mike Warnke.[27] For the last decade and a half, at least, Larson has focused on "spiritual warfare," specializing in what he declares to be deliverance from evil spirits. The Spiritual Warfare movement is, in this context, an Evangelical/Charismatic spawned notion rooted in traditional Christian Demonology and practice.

One could think of it as a Fundamentalist Protestant take on *The Exorcist*!

According to the Wikipedia article on "Spiritual Warfare":

---

[25] Dizdar's website is a melange of articles and events such as the "Occult Satanic Crimes Conference." See: http://goo.gl/BBDTeq.

[26] Bob Larson, *UFO's and the Alien Agenda: Uncovering the Mystery Behind UFO's and the Paranormal* (Thomas Nelson, Inc., 1997).

[27] Warnke is a Christian evangelist whose self-proclaimed role as an expert on the subject of Satanism was debunked when his claims of having been a Satanist high priest were thoroughly discredited by the Christian magazine, *Cornerstone*. John Trott and Mike Hertenstein, "Selling Satan: The Tragic History of Mike Warnke," *Cornerstone* 21, No. 98, 1992.

In evangelism and worldwide Christian missions, former missionaries such as Charles Kraft and C. Peter Wagner have emphasized problems with demonic influences on the world mission fields and the need to drive demons out. Robert Guelich of Fuller Theological Seminary has questioned the extent to which spiritual warfare has shifted from its basic moorings from being a metaphor for the Christian life. He underlines how spiritual warfare has evolved into "spiritual combat" techniques for Christians to seek power over demons. Guelich argues that Paul's writings in the Epistle to the Ephesians are focused on proclaiming the peace of God and nowhere specify any techniques for battling demons. He also finds that the novels of Frank Peretti are seriously at odds with both the gospel narratives on demons and Pauline teaching.[28]

To put it in fairly generous terms, aspects of the "spiritual warfare" motif flirt with the edges of orthodoxy in that they diverge from traditional Christian scripture and practice. From the perspective of my own beliefs and interpretations of Christianity, there certainly seems to exist here an absence of the things which make Christianity intrinsically Christian, such as the Cross, the Resurrection, grace, forgiveness, love, and all of the other aspects that are difficult about our faith. These are the elements that draw us to our fellow humans rather than viewing them as the

---

[28] Yes, despite what I sometimes tell my students not to do, I'm citing Wikipedia. Despite its flaws, it's useful for broad overviews and especially as a starting point for exploring subjects more deeply. "Spiritual Warfare," *Wikipedia*, http://goo.gl/WOc4eP.

enemy in some fundamental, soul-level manner.

But what about the space aliens? There's a connection between perceiving the existence of demonic, palpable evil in human form, and exhibiting paranoia over phenomena such as "alien" abductions. It always struck me as odd that the crossover between the "Devil Fear" and the "Alien Fear" actually took so long to occur. After all, the beginning of the saucer contact mythos had strong spiritual overtones, even though these did not fit exactly with orthodox, traditional religious dogmas. The stories of the Contactees often referred to some sort of universal Cosmic Law, and a god or spirit which was shared by humanity as well as the Space Brothers. Early concerns about the possibility of intelligent extraterrestrial life having an adverse effect on our religious culture indicated that, as far back as the Brookings report, the overlap in the two topics was contemplated.[29] As the scientific bent of 1960s saucer research took hold these religious questions were relegated to the back burner. Writers such as John Keel and Jacques Vallee did much to move the notion of a more holistic ufology back to the fore, but serious discussions of the intersection between religion and the paranormal were the exception rather than the rule.

Regardless of one's views on religion in general, or on

---

[29] See U.S. House of Representatives, 87th Congress, First Session, Report of the Committee on Science and Astronautics, H.Rpt. 66831, "Proposed Studies on the Implications of Peaceful Space Activities for Human Affairs," Washington, U.S. Government Printing Office, 1961, http://goo.gl/nNNhrj. Although the report (colloquially referred to as the "Brookings Report") discussed the need for research on many policy issues related to space exploration, it is most often cited for passages from its brief section on the implications of a discovery of extraterrestrial life.

specific faiths or denominations, the connections between the spiritual and the paranormal *are* there. It's just awkward and difficult to look at it for any length of time. Like the intersection of the paranormal and academia, any conclusions one draws tend to alienate at least half of the audience. But maybe it's time for that to change.

I believe that the collaboration between evangelical fundamentalism and the paranormal, which I've taken to calling the para-evangelical fringe, tends to undermine each of the component belief systems. The philosophy, theology, ethic of service to others and, above all, the notion of God's all-consuming grace that have been part of Christianity since its beginning are sublimated to an over-emphasis on eschatology and demonology. The mystery and wonder of the paranormal, as well as the importance of rational observation and study, are reduced to a supporting role as the para-evangelicals use the various manifestations of the paranormal (especially aliens and ghosts) as props in their attempt to push various political agendas, often at the expense of the Protestant Churches' traditional core message of salvation.

Mainstream Protestantism has had an interesting relationship with the paranormal, particularly the UFO phenomenon, over the past sixty years. The reactions range from polite interest to scholarly study, but one consistent theme has been that whatever the UFOs may be, the focus of Christians should be on the Cross, and on Christ. The fringe of the fundamentalist wing of Protestantism, on the other hand, has – as a part of its worldview – developed a complex system of eschatological thought. This worldview attempts to interpret Old and New Testament prophetic writings in light of current events in order to gauge the imminence of the "End Times." Some within that wing of Evangelical Protestantism have integrated the paranormal into their various "end of the world" scenarios.

In this chapter I am coming at these issues from the perspective of a believing Christian. As a result, I no doubt give more credence to Christian scriptures and theories than a non-Christian would. I acknowledge that this is far from a skeptical position, but I believe that this "Space Demon" trend has a deleterious effect on Christian thought. As a Christian, one of the most disturbing aspects of the alien-as-demon trope is the pervasive assumption that the alleged aliens are beyond Christ's salvation. If the aliens are intelligent, sentient beings then they should – at least according to my understanding of Christian theology – be just as susceptible to God's Spirit working faith within them as any other sentient creature. Of course, they would have the choice to reject God's grace, as do we all. The notion, however, that alien beings are demonic raises crucial questions about this salvation. Can fallen angels change their minds, so to speak, and be saved? Among those Christians who believe this to be a question which actually merits consideration, the answer is no. One example of this line of thought is presented on "The Watcher Website," authored by David Flynn:

> Jesus Christ is called the KINSMAN REDEEMER. Jesus did not come to save the apes & dolphins, He did not come to save the puppies & kitties, and He certainly did not come to save the Zeta Reticulans or the Alien Grays. The atonement work of Jesus was only to save His kinsman, the sons of Adam. If a being is not a descendent of Adam, this being – no matter how intelligent – will not take part in the promise of Jesus Christ. Watcher's research confirms that there are beings who are genetically similar to the race of Adams, but

have been genetically tampered with by rebel angels, or engineered to be superior humans in some illuminated laboratory. These hybrids are not capable of "being saved" by the grace of the Kinsman Redeemer, for they are not His kinsman... This increase in seemingly humans who are not genetically sons of Adam is a symptom of the end times, just as in the days of Noah when Nephilim walked the earth among humans. If Christians are speculating whether or not aliens can be saved, they are just adding to the confusion. "Aliens" are really disembodied angels – the rebellious angels who according to Jude left their God-given habitation to dwell in genetically manipulated hybrid bodies just prior to the Flood... the Nephilim of Genesis 6.[30]

The reference to the Epistle of Jude appears in verse six of the brief letter: "And the angels who did not keep their positions of authority but abandoned their proper dwelling – these he has kept in darkness, bound with everlasting chains for judgment on the great Day."[31] As Flynn points out, this verse does refer to some angels leaving the "positions of authority." Jude does not discuss hybrids. The Epistle of Jude is, however, significant in this culture of demons and aliens. Of all New Testament writers, Jude provides the most prominent reference to apocryphal writings such as the Book of Enoch. Since the Book of Enoch is one of the key texts that discusses the Nephilim,

[30] "UFOs & the Bible: Genesis 6 & Nephilim 101," *The Watcher*, http://goo.gl/QMMRzh.

[31] *New International Version Bible*, Jude 1:6. http://goo.gl/8G40Sw.

the human-other hybrids briefly mentioned in the sixth chapter of Genesis, this second-hand canonicity has fueled the demon/alien conversation and lent a near-Biblical credence to the concept.

Regardless of the factual, literal veracity of human-demon hybrids masquerading as space aliens, I am more concerned with the attitude of those who believe potential non-human sentient beings – even fallen angels – are beyond salvation. To declare someone – *anyone* – to be beyond salvation is to place limits upon the power and love of God. I'm not entirely sure that's a particularly Christian thing to do. In many ways, however, this attitude fits in the world of the para-evangelical fringe, which is devoted to the acquisition of power – spiritual, economic, and political.

Russ Dizdar, in particular, is fascinating to me. His work draws on a wide variety of extant theories and tales that include spiritual warfare. His Project Josiah initiative, for example, is self-described as, "A serious call to strategic spiritual warfare, intercession, world evangelization, exposing and engaging the rise of dark powers."[32] This is combined with the old bugaboos of Satanic Ritual Abuse, MK-Ultra, top secret mind-controlled super soldier programs, "the occult" and the like. As you might expect, if you've read this far, the atemporality of Russ Dizdar is striking.

We may define the atemporal as eruptions of the past (and future) in the present – a world where the linear nature

---

[32] "Project Josiah" is self-described on their website as follows: "Project Josiah was a prayer ministry that was started from Shatter the Darkness ministry to call prayer warriors to pray against Bohemian Grove and dark satanic works." Among other "resources" they feature on their website, one can find "Warfare Prayer" MP3 audio files for use as inspiration. See: http://www.projectjosiah.com/.

of time is ignored. From the historian's point of view, what this does is remove events, concepts, and theories from their natural historical context. When people like Dizdar discuss the MK-Ultra project as though it is an ongoing issue, responsible for events such as the Aurora, Colorado and Newtown, Connecticut mass shootings, they are removing that project (which was very real) from the moorings of its actual context. Subject to such use, "MK Ultra" changes meaning. It goes from being a CIA project lasting in various forms from the early 1950s to the early 1970s, to shorthand for far more reaching generic evil government-sponsored mind control activities.[33]

Dizdar is careful to draw a distinction between the "traditional" Satanism of Anton LaVey and what he calls "The Brotherhood"- multigenerational "bloodline" groups of Satan worshiping bad guys. He also hits the high points of conspiracy theories that have emerged since the MK-Ultra revelations of the 1970s and the Satanic ritual abuse paranoia of the 1980s. Finally, he folds in the New World Order multinational Illuminati conspiracies of the 1990s

---

[33] Project MK Ultra was the code name of a covert human research operation by the United States government that experimented in the behavioral engineering of humans through the CIA's Scientific Intelligence Division. The program began in the early 1950s, was officially sanctioned in 1953, and was finally officially halted in 1973. The program engaged in many illegal activities, in particular the use of unwitting American and Canadian citizens as its test subjects. U.S. Senate, 95th Congress, 1st Session, Select Committee on Intelligence and the Subcommittee on Health and Scientific Research of the Committee on Human Resources, "Project MKUltra, the Central Intelligence Agency's Program of Research into Behavioral Modification," Washington, D.C., U.S. Government Printing Office, 1977, http://goo.gl/En8bG6.

and the Bohemian Grove-Power Elite suspicions which gained prominence in the first decade of the 21st century. It is a mind-boggling stew of modern conspiracy theory.

Obviously, Dizdar is not the first to discuss any of these things, but that's the point. His work remixes decades of theories and fears. Sometimes the details are updated to make them more relevant to the current era (Aurora and Newtown taking the place of Columbine in the "mind controlled mass killer" narrative, for example), but the bones of his story are consistent with what has been extant in the paranormal field for decades.

Cathy O'Brien's *Trance Formation of America* is clearly the starting point for much of the "generational" mind control material.[34] New Age/Conspiracy writer Ron Garman, who wrote under the pseudonym "Gurudas" until his death in 2001, was saying almost identical things about mind controlled assassins on late night radio in the mid-1990s.[35]

While Dizdar's stories have the added feature of numerous anecdotes of these mind-controlled government/Satanic assassins attacking him and his family, there is much that is derivative. That a global conspiracy run by Satan himself is unable to take out a single C-list

---

[34] Cathy O'Brien and Mark Phillips, *Trance Formation of America* (Reality Marketing, Inc., 1995). O'Brien is an American who claims to be a victim of a mind control government project named Project Monarch, which she said was part of the CIA's Project MKULTRA. A copy of the book can be found on-line at: http://goo.gl/hyl9zc.

[35] Gurudas, *Treason: The New World Order* (Cassandra Press, 1996). Garman was a frequent guest on conspiracy-oriented radio shows such as The Jeff Rense Program. A 1996 appearance of Garman on the Rense program can be heard at: http://youtu.be/MJKeGL5UN70.

paranormal personality is amusing.[36] Dizdar, of course, attributes his continued survival to the fact that God is personally protecting him in his efforts to expose this looming threat.

Dizdar's riffs on the paranormal-as-demonic genre have been effective because they appeal to overlapping and interrelated demographic groups. Political paranoiacs, fundamentalist Evangelicals, and devotees of "Hidden History" have all found something to grab on to in Dizdar's work. That does not make his claims false, but it is far more fascinating to me to explore the roots of such claims rather than to simply denounce them.

The Seven Hills Dominionism of groups like the supposed Collins Elite combines the worlds of the political and the paranormal (if, indeed, those are separate worlds; my particular jury is still out on that). To some observers, current cultural trends are clearly demonic (or at least broadly sinful). Thus their attempts to push back against what they see as anti-Christian secularism is a form of spiritual warfare, conducted at the ballot box rather than in the exorcist's chamber. Often the theology and Christianity of these groups tends to take a back seat to their politics.

In a nutshell, the basic idea behind "Seven Hills Dominionism" is to place Christians – by which they generally mean their particular flavor of Evangelical Protestant Christians, rather than Catholics, Quakers, Greek Orthodox, and so on – in positions of power in a variety of places in the political and cultural life of the United States (and eventually the whole planet), including religion, government, and entertainment. According to one organization, "The American Vision" (whose paradoxical

---

[36] Lest anyone accuse me of a status-based snobbery here, I'd like to point out that I'm not on any paranormal personality list at all.

slogan is "Exercising Servanthood Dominion"), their goal is the establishment of, "An America that recognizes the sovereignty of God over all of life, where Christians apply a Biblical worldview to every facet of society. This future America will be again a 'city on a hill' drawing all nations to the Lord Jesus Christ and teaching them to subdue the earth for the advancement of His Kingdom."[37]

The notion of God's Kingdom (and attempts to bring it about on Earth) is a recurring one in Dominionist literature. In 2011, "spiritual warfare" theologian C. Peter Wagner described Dominionism in this way:

> One of the things He does want He taught us to pray for in the Lord's Prayer: "Your kingdom come, Your will be done on earth as it is in heaven." This means that we do our best to see that what we know is characteristic of heaven work its way into the warp and woof of our society here on earth. Think of heaven: no injustice, no poverty, righteousness, peace, prosperity, no disease, love, no corruption, no crime, no misery, no racism, and I could go on. Wouldn't you like your city to display those characteristics? But where does dominion come in? On the first page of the Bible, God told Adam and Eve to "fill the earth and subdue it; have dominion over the fish of the sea, etc." (Genesis 1:28). Adam, Eve, and the whole human race were to take dominion over the rest of creation, but Satan entered the picture, succeeded in usurping Adam's dominion for himself and became what Jesus calls "the ruler

---

[37] *The American Vision: A Biblical Worldview Ministry*, The American Vision, Inc., http://americanvision.org/about/.

of this world" (John 14:30). When Jesus came, he brought the kingdom of God and He expects His kingdom-minded people to take whatever action is needed to push back the long-standing kingdom of Satan and bring the peace and prosperity of His kingdom here on earth. This is what we mean by dominionism.[38]

There is a lot going on in this selection that is emblematic of the dominionist movement as a whole. There is an assumption throughout that the will of God is to establish a kingdom in perfect alignment with what Christians would recognize as "good." When Wagner describes Heaven in terms of a perfect paradise, his examples are rooted in earthly notions. If Heaven is truly the realm of God, then human concepts of racism, injustice, and so on, would not be part of that universe. It is not that they would merely be absent: the concepts themselves would not exist. The dominionist notion of God's kingdom simply being an idealized Earth is therefore, in my opinion, woefully simplistic.

A more traditional interpretation of the "Thy Kingdom come" section of the Lord's Prayer can be seen in Martin Luther's Small Catechism:

> "Thy kingdom come." *What does this mean?* The kingdom of God comes indeed without our prayer, of itself; but we pray in this petition that it may come unto us also. *How is this done?* When our heavenly Father gives us His Holy Spirit, so that by His grace we believe His Holy Word and lead a godly life here in time and

[38] C. Peter Wagner, "The New Apostolic Reformation," *Global Spheres*, 18 August 2011, http://goo.gl/qAL8PL.

yonder in eternity.[39]

This interpretation is less worldly, and more personal and ethereal. Luther's interpretation of this phrase – though it originated in the 16th century – is rooted in the western Christian tradition. It must also be noted that while Luther was the source of a great deal of disruption in the relatively narrow world of western European theology, he was a very conservative figure with regard to politics. He roundly denounced, for example, assertions that the Reformation should extend to a restructuring of the social and political orders.

The notion of Christianity being the dominant cultural and political force of a nation or kingdom is not new. In the West, it goes back to Rome, and the declaration by Emperor Theodosius I in 380 CE that Nicene Christianity was the official doctrine of the Empire.[40] In the United States, however, it is a relatively recent phenomenon, with its genesis in the twentieth century, despite rhetoric that refers to cities on hills and America's Christian heritage. American Vision lists the following seven hills – or mountains – as being targets of this new "Christian" takeover: business, government, family, religion, media, education, and entertainment. They argue that they are merely "restoring" America to its biblical foundations, but upon looking deeper there is a strong political objective rather than one which is purely theological.

In the "county rights" section of the American Vision

---

[39] Martin Luther, "Luther's Little Instruction Book (The Small Catechism of Martin Luther)," Trans. by Robert E. Smith, *Project Wittenberg*, 22 May 1994, http://goo.gl/TM1WYu.

[40] Stephen Williams and Gerard Friell, *Theodosius: The Empire at Bay* (B. T. Batsford, Ltd., 1994), 47 – 54.

website the organization explores the loss of "American freedom" which they contend dates from the ratification of the Constitution and its replacement of the Articles of Confederation. According to American Vision, this resulted in greater authority for a centralized, national government at the expense of the states. Thus, the rot set in early. As Joel McDurmon writes on the American Vision website:

> We cannot solve the problem if we are continually trying to fix the wrong problem. We cannot plan a proper solution to the problem if we are misstating the problem, or stating only part of it. For example, we feel free to condemn Wilson or FDR, Johnson or Obama, Socialism or the Fed, and yet we remain timid or even defiantly opposed to criticizing even parts of the Constitution itself. But if the Constitution was the first great act of centralization in this land – the act which enabled and empowered all subsequent centralization in this country (exactly as predicted by its opponents) – then it will do little good to clear away the subsequent acts alone. If the root remains viable, the brambles will grow back. "Return to the Constitution" sounds nice, but what good does it do to return ourselves atop the same slippery slope we've already gone down.[41]

To American Vision, centralization under state and federal governments, rather than other problems, is the true source of all challenges confronting the United States. The

---

[41] Joel McDurmon, "State's Rights: how they were lost (in part)," *The American Vision*, 26 August 2011. http://goo.gl/IKjTos.

only solution is the application of theonomy, or the ruling of a state in accordance with divine law. This differs slightly from theocracy, in which a state is ruled by the divine figure him/her/itself (presumably through an earthly religious structure).

The stance espoused by American Vision and their fellow travelers is in stark contrast to long-standing Christian tradition, which goes back at least to St. Augustine's *City of God*, of the temporal/physical/political world existing in a separate sphere than the eternal/spiritual world. This doctrine of Two Cities (or Kingdoms) is well expressed by Michael Horton:

> In our Christian circles in the United States today, we can discern a "Christendom" view, where some imagine America to be a Christian nation invested with a divine commission to bring freedom to the ends of the earth. Of course, Christians have an obligation both to proclaim the heavenly and everlasting freedom of the Gospel and the earthly and temporal freedom from injustice. But they are different. When we confuse them, we take the kingdom into our own hands, transforming it from a kingdom of grace into a kingdom of glory and power.[42]

The notion of power arises again and again in the words of the dominionists, whether in terms of political power, spiritual warfare or any other realm.

This all relates back to the paranormal. To a certain degree, we can consider religion as one category of

---

[42] Michael Horton, "A Tale of Two Kingdoms," *Ligonier Ministries*, http://goo.gl/DgxnWs.

paranormal thought and activity. Many have sought to align various types of religious and paranormal experiences, from visitations to "missing time", in an attempt to reconcile the two subcultures.[43] I think the similarities extend from the nature of these phenomena to the uses of them by their experiencers. Both are deeply personal, and often the personal meaning of these experiences and beliefs are very difficult to convey to those who have no stake in them.

Sadly, the greedy, unstable, and amoral within the institutional structures of both religion and the paranormal have used these points of convergence as a set of emotionally affecting tools to take advantage of the credulous and damaged. In the end, however, the havoc and pain wrought by both unscrupulous purveyors of the paranormal and religion have done less to weaken my faith in God or fascination with the paranormal than to weaken my faith in humanity and its ability to engage with the unknown, and unknowable.

---

[43] See, for example, Paul Kimball, *The Other Side of Truth: The Paranormal, The Art of the Imagination, and the Human Condition* (Redstar Books, 2012), pp. 1 – 8.

CHAPTER FIVE

THE STRANGE JOURNEY OF WILD BILL COOPER

Perhaps no figure from 1980s and 1990s ufology affected my initial thinking on the subject more than the late William Cooper. Cooper remains a significant figure in the paranormal and conspiracy worlds for a variety of reasons, including his contribution to the dark and paranoid mythologies springing from the advent of the Majestic 12 (MJ-12) documents. His most lasting, and in my opinion damaging, contribution to "the field" was his role as one of the key links between ufology and right-wing political paranoia, including the so-called "Militia" movement.

On a personal level, it was the work of William Cooper that I first encountered when I poked my head into the paranormal corners of the Internet back in 1994. By that time, he had gone from established figure to a bit of an outsider – his initial emergence onto the UFO cover up scene in the late 1980s produced much of his most memorable material – but I could not stop reading his work. There was a passion and anger, along with a visceral fear present in his words. It was evangelistic: Cooper's "Gospel" was dark and frightening, full of complex connections between people, organizations, and nations, and it called us to initiation into the hidden truths of how the world *really* worked. Cooper was angry and afraid, of the space aliens as well as their dupes in the coming New World Order, and his mission seemed to be to make his readers just as angry and afraid.[44]

It certainly worked with me.

Milton William "Bill" Cooper first burst onto the UFO scene in the late 1980s, following the "revelations" of John Lear, the O. H. Krill documents, Val Valerian's MATRIX document, and other ephemera which tied into the promotion of the MJ-12 documents.[45] The supporters of these documents initially consisted of Roswell researchers Stanton Friedman and William Moore, along with television producer Jaime Shandera. They asserted that the MJ-12 documents proved the existence of a secret working group to deal with extraterrestrials that had been established within the US government after the alleged crash of an alien spacecraft near Roswell, New Mexico, in 1947.[46] Extrapolations of these documents led to scenarios in which the American government had entered into an agreement with the aliens to trade human experimental

[44] Milton William Cooper, *Behold a Pale Horse* (Light Technology Publishing, 1991). *Behold a Pale Horse* was Cooper's magnum opus, and it remains a touchstone for the fringes of the conspiracy subculture.

[45] Valdemar Valerian (aka John Grace), *The Matrix: Understanding Aspects of Covert Interaction with Alien Culture, Technology and Planetary Power* (Arcturus Book Services, 1988); O. H. Krill (aka John Grace), "A Situation Report on Our Acquisition of Advanced Technology and Interaction with Alien Cultures," January 1988, http://goo.gl/m9Q9mB.

[46] Stanton T. Friedman, *Top Secret / MAJIC* (Marlowe & Company, 1996). For a good general survey of Moore, Friedman, Shandera, and the history of the MJ-12 saga, see the discussion between Greg Bishop and Paul Kimball at "Birds of a Feather," *The Other Side of Truth Podcast*, Kimball Media, July 2012, http://goo.gl/DhmLMm.

subjects for advanced technology. If you ever watched *The X-Files* or were one of the dozen or so people like me who followed NBC's underrated series *Dark Skies*, you probably absorbed some of this mythology without realizing it.[47]

Cooper claimed that he had access to top secret information about extraterrestrial contact and associated conspiracies when he had been an enlisted man in the US Navy. He asserted that his pursuit of the truth had cost him jobs and that he had been threatened by shadowy, Men in Black type figures. Like many people at the time, Cooper interacted with others in the fledgling online scene surrounding these issues at such venues as Paranet, a BBS (Bulletin Board System) accessed with dial-up modems. Later, the key conversations on the "alien question" would move to the Internet, first on e-mail and UseNet, and later on the World Wide Web.

Cooper emerged onto the scene in 1989 with a grandiosely titled paper, "The Secret Government: The Origin, Identity, and Purpose of MJ-12." In this document, he attempted to put together the pieces of various extraterrestrial-themed conspiracies and in the process presumably make some sort of name for himself.[48]

The drive to present a story in which one assembles all possible bits of evidence (or purported evidence) into a unified whole is one of the most compelling aspects of conspiracy writing. In the world of paranoia and conspiracy there can be no ambiguity, and there must be nothing out of place. Anything that *is* out of place must, of necessity,

---

[47] For a good chronology of Cooper's activities, see Don Ecker, "Dark Days Revisited: Chaos in the UFO Underground," *UFO Magazine*, February / March 2002.

[48] William Milton Cooper, "The Secret Government: The Origin, Identity, and Purpose of MJ-12," http://goo.gl/hc4kQw.

either be reconciled and integrated into the conspiracy, or disregarded.

Although Cooper made much of his insider knowledge as a member of the "Intelligence Briefing Team," the bulk of his commentary and theories were drawn from extant sources, including the classic 1988 online posting of the Krill documents and the Matrix writings of Val Valerian. One example of this is the handling of the death of Secretary of Defense James Forrestal. The Krill document addresses it thusly:

> The MJ-12 group has been a continuously existing group since it was created, with new members replacing others that die. For example, when Secretary Forrestal was upset at seeing the United States sold out in World War II, he wound up being sent to a Naval hospital for emotional strain. Before relatives could get to him, he "jumped out a 16th story window." Most persons close to him consider his suicide contrived. When Forrestal died, he was replaced by General Walter B. Smith.[49]

Cooper was one of the first to present the Krill papers to a wide audience on various BBS sites. Building on the information in the Krill documents, the "Origin and Identity of MJ-12" document addressed and expanded on various topics raised in the earlier document. This included Forrestal's death, but Cooper painted it in much more lurid terms.

James Forrestal did indeed experience psychological difficulties in the late 1940s and did, in fact, die under

---

[49] Krill, Ibid.

circumstances which have been surrounded in controversy. There are also, interestingly, a number of conspiracy theories surrounding his death that have *nothing* to do with extraterrestrials or the paranormal. The most prominent of these revolve around KGB shenanigans, or relate to Forrestal's opposition to the partition of Palestine. Cooper's contribution was to connect the death explicitly to the alien cover up, a connection that continues to be made to this day by conspiracists within the UFO subculture.[50]

Although this is not exclusive to Cooper's work, the attempt to fold Forrestal's death into the broader alien cover-up narrative was another example of the compulsion to impose order on the chaos which fills our world. To a conspiracist such as Cooper, someone like James Forrestal couldn't just succumb to psychological and medical problems. There's a bizarre sort of "status consciousness" that goes along with this line of thinking. Those in

---

[50] Cooper, "Origin, Identity, and purpose of MJ-12." Cooper wrote: "Secretary of Defense James Forrestal began to object to the secrecy [surrounding the US government's dealings with extraterrestrials]… Sometime in the early morning of May 22, 1949 agents of the CIA tied a sheet around his neck, fastened the other end to a fixture in his room and threw James Forrestal out the window. The sheet tore and he plummeted to his death. He became one of the first victims of the cover-up." As an example of how this meme has continued, see, for example, Peter Robbins, "MJ-12 and the Strange Death of James Forrestal," *2004 X-Conference Proceedings*, Lost Arts Media, Video, 2004. The introduction to the lecture is available on video at http://youtu.be/EJNuA-cFjx0; the text can be found re-printed at http://goo.gl/iSBk3W. The echoes of William Cooper can be heard when Robbins states, "The murder of James Forrestal was simply the only way to guarantee the resolution of what this group had come to perceive as a potential security risk of the first magnitude."

positions of power are, somehow, not subject to the same bad luck that the rest of us may experience. A heart attack is never *just* a heart attack if you're a cabinet official. Every car accident is intentional; every illness is the result of skullduggery.[51]

Another key component of Cooper's interpretation and presentation of the MJ-12 conspiracy was his emphasis on topics that are prominent in the worlds of extremist right-wing political paranoia, rather than the more apolitical manifestations of the extraterrestrial version.[52]

The REX-84 military exercises have made appearances in a number of conspiracy theories over the years. The name of the plan was short for Readiness Exercise 1984,

---

[51] UFO conspiracist and fringe historian Richard Dolan, for example, has speculated that UFO researcher Dr. James E. McDonald may have been murdered because of his UFO activities. McDonald committed suicide in 1971, after a failed first attempt had left him blinded. There is no evidence that his death involved anything nefarious. Richard Dolan, *UFOs & The National Security State: Chronology of a Cover-Up, 1941 – 1973* (Hampton Roads, 2002), 380 – 382.

[52] Cooper, "Origin, Identity, and purpose of MJ-12." For example, Cooper wrote, "The Government will… suspend the Constitution and declare martial law. The secret alien army of implanted humans and all dissidents, which translates into anyone they choose, will be rounded up and placed in the one-mile-square concentration camps which already exist. Are the people whom they intend to place in these concentration camps destined to make up the reported "batch consignments" of slave labor needed by the space colonies? The media – radio, TV, newspapers, and computer networks – will be nationalized and seized. Anyone who resists will be taken or killed. This entire operation was rehearsed by the government and military in 1984 under the code name REX-84A and it went off without a hitch."

which was a secretive "scenario and drill" developed by the United States federal government to suspend the United States Constitution, declare martial law, place military commanders in charge of state and local governments, and detain large numbers of American citizens who are deemed to be "national security threats," in the event that the President declares a "State of National Emergency."[53]

This operation first came to widespread public attention during the 1987 Iran-Contra hearings when Representative Jack Brooks questioned Lieutenant Colonel Oliver North about his role in developing the plan. REX 84 was far from unique in American history. Throughout the twentieth century, there had been government contingency plans to sequester, imprison, or otherwise remove potential troublemakers, be they Japanese-Americans, Communists, Hippies, Black Power advocates, or opponents of potential American military intervention in Central America, as was apparently the case with REX 84. By the late 1980s and early 1990s the radical fringe of the right wing of American politics believed they were the next targets of the federal government.[54]

Thus, with Cooper's writing, and the writing of those he championed, came one of the first and most enduring connections between the paranormal and political conspiracy theories and paranoia. Since the 1950s there had been rumors and fears of government intimidation of UFO witnesses, but this was different. What Cooper and his ilk promoted was the idea that the government, or at least powerful forces controlling the government, had extensive

[53] "Rex 84," *Wikipedia*, http://en.wikipedia.org/wiki/Rex_84.

[54] Ward Churchill and Jim Vanderwall, *The COINTELPRO Papers: Documents from the FBI's Secret Wars Against Dissent in the United States* (South End Press, 2001), 410 – 411.

plans for rounding up, imprisoning, and possibly executing millions of Americans that they deemed to be dangerous. It didn't matter if you had seen a flying saucer or not. These weren't the Men in Black of Albert Bender and Gray Barker, coming to warn you to shut up after you wrote something in a flying saucer 'zine; these were stormtroopers bundling you off to a concentration camp. Cooper's prophecies invoked the specter of pure totalitarian oppression.

Cooper formed his own organization, the Civilian Agency for Joint Intelligence (CAJI). Occasionally, material would appear on the on-line CAJI discussion board that was significant enough to survive on various archival sites (like textiles.com) into the Internet Age. This is, sadly, the only way to relive the wild and wooly days of the late 1980s and early to mid 1990s.[55]

There was definitely hedging and self-aggrandizement – a contributor to the mythology (or "the truth," depending on your point of view) could only be *as* important as Cooper was, certainly not more. These posts, regardless of their original source, also served to underline Cooper's fundamental and lasting vision: a paranoid panorama,

---

[55] When such entries appeared, Cooper would often provide a self-serving preface, such as the following: "NOTE! This file was uploaded to CAJI by a user on July 5, 1990. The source of the information is unknown at the present time. I can verify much of the information as true and correct and is information that could not have been known by anyone other than someone like me who has worked very closely with the truth… It was obviously written by someone who has access to the same Top Secret information to which I also had access." This introduction could be summarized much more succinctly: "Here's some stuff; it may be a lie; I saw some stuff too; I'm important." William Cooper, "CAJI," July 1990, http://goo.gl/X0rJU2.

dominated by the threat of the United States Government's growing power and that of overt and covert multinational organizations. The July 5, 1990 file which Cooper introduced above was filled with information about reptilians, mothmen, and the assassinations of men like James Forrestal who "tried to reveal the truth" about the American/alien collusion.

The result was a breathtaking kaleidoscopic mélange of 20th century conspiracism. In one posting, for example, it was posited that the flourishing of the illicit drug economy was the result of a government plot. Like many conspiracy theories, this was rooted in a sort of reality.[56] But the "intel" from CAJI took the notion of extralegal drug smuggling out of its plausible realm of money laundering and influencing international politics and placed it in the more paranoid milieu of social control experimentation. Along the way references were made to monetary policy ("the coming currency call-in") and warnings that the US government would soon declare martial law. Eventually, of course, this digression into drug policy and domestic paranoia connected back into the larger issue of extraterrestrial visitation and collusion between the aliens and the US government. As with everything else, it was just another thread in the grand tapestry of the space alien conspiracy.

The warped genius of Cooper was his ability to blend a number of disparate memes that originally emerged in different contexts into a narrative that many found compelling. This is another example of the "remix culture" that I discussed at the beginning of this book. Cooper deftly melded paranormal and political paranoia and

---

[56] Peter Dale Scott and Jonathan Marshall, *Cocaine Politics: Drugs, Armies, and the CIA in Central America* (University of California Press, 1998).

conspiracies so thoroughly that it became difficult to determine where one aspect ended and the other began.

In the mid-to-late 1990s, however, Cooper's tone shifted. The paranormal began to take a back seat to his political and (broadly speaking) occult fears and theories. Cooper's apotheosis came with the publication of *Behold a Pale Horse*, a 1991 compilation of his online writings and text of his speeches. Along with Cooper's writing the book included:

- facsimiles of redacted government documents;
- facsimiles of think tank reports;
- facsimiles of various conspiracy newsletters;
- facsimiles of Cooper's military records;
- a facsimile of the *Protocols of the Elders of Zion* (which was not really about the Jews, according to Cooper);
- facsimiles of correspondence between Cooper and a variety of individuals;
- facsimiles of correspondence between various other people; and
- facsimiles of newspaper articles.[57]

Despite the fact that at least half of the book consisted of reproductions of other people's work, Cooper had the temerity to assert at the beginning of the volume that, "The ideas and conclusions expressed in this work are mine alone."

One can still find *Behold a Pale Horse* in online as well as

[57] Cooper, *Behold a Pale Horse*.

brick-and-mortar bookstores, and time has not dimmed the feeling, when handling the book, that one is in possession of information one should not have, as if it were a kind of conspiracist *Necronomicon*. Despite its hodgepodge, scrapbook-like nature – or perhaps because of it – it is a very impressive, important looking volume. The design rhetoric of the book evoked a feeling that one was in the process of acquiring some kind of transgressive knowledge. For some of us, there is a certain frisson that comes from seeing redacted, blacked out text in a government document. Regardless of the importance or significance of the words blacked out, the very fact that it was blacked out is exciting. One of the goofiest, but effective touches in the design was a footer which read:

****T O P S E C R E T ****

It was at the bottom of *each* page. Of course, none of the information in the book *was* top secret (or any other kind of "secret"), but such touches made the reader feel special; we were members of an elite group who had stumbled across something we really shouldn't have discovered. As a marketing ploy, even if an unintentional one, it was brilliant.

While *Behold a Pale Horse* offers a précis of Cooper's views at the height of his BBS notoriety, the key document for understanding Cooper's point of view at the end of his career (and his life) is simply called "MAJESTYTWELVE." The name itself was quite clever. Cooper stated that this was the name of "a set of Top Secret documents" he saw while in the US Navy. Notice the similarity to MJ-12, which had by then become a ufological mainstay. Cooper's mysterious document was close enough to generate a kind of mythic resonance but *just* different enough that he could maintain a position of being original and distinct from the pack.

MAJESTYTWELVE is a rollicking tale of how everything is seemingly connected to a shadowy group of elites who have existed since the dawn of recorded history. Their intentions, it goes without saying, are not in humanity's best interest. Much of the text of this seminal 1997 document was familiar to those of us who had followed Cooper's exploits to one degree or another over the years, particularly those of us who had read *Behold a Pale Horse*. But there was a new and shocking twist, summarized in this snippet:

> For many years I sincerely believed that an extraterrestrial threat existed and that it was the most important driving force behind world events. I was wrong and for that I most deeply and humbly apologize.[58]

A recantation of this sort was almost unheard of amongst the ranks of the ufological subculture. Cooper's conspiratorial viewpoint had clearly shifted. Now, instead of prominent ufologists being engaged in a campaign of disinformation to cover up the truth about alien visitation, prominent ufologists were instead engaged in a campaign of disinformation to convince people that UFOs actually existed. Not since Dylan went electric had there been such a complete volte face!

Why would they do this, asked Cooper? The answer was simple: To promote the emergence of the totalitarian New World Order:

> Socialist change agents known to you as

---

[58] Milton William Cooper, "MAJESTYTWELVE," *Hour of the Time*, 1997, http://goo.gl/W2IQdX.

William Moore, Jaime Shandera, and Stanton T. Friedman presented the hoax known as Operation Majestic-12. These fake documents were printed in the socialist New York Times. It was an attempt to lead the sheople away from the truth by presenting an artificial alien threat as a "government cover-up" of extraterrestrial visitation. Most of the well known uFOOLogists and so-called UFO researchers are Illuminati, Marxist, CIA, or KGB change agents operating in furtherance of propagandizing the American People.[59]

In Cooper's new revelation, "Majestic-12" was in fact a hoax perpetrated by the shadow government, of which people like Friedman were devious double-dealing disinformation agents. Cooper's radical far right wing political ideology shone through in his new work. Socialism and Marxism were clearly a threat as were both the CIA and the KGB. The "War of the Worlds" hoax perpetrated by Orson Welles was also a part of this attempt to present a credible alien threat, but the technology did not exist in the 1930s to fully implement the plan.

What was "the plan"? Well, according to Cooper the powers-that-be were going to present an alien threat to encourage people (or "sheople" as he called them) to abrogate their liberty and accept a dictatorial global government. Also part of the effort to implement world socialism was the demonization of the following groups:

Fundamentalist Christians, Jews, Moslems, the lawful Militia, and anyone else who might fight in defense of the Constitution or Freedom.

[59] Cooper, "MAJESTYTWELVE."

> These terrorist acts deliver a message to the American People that any opposition to the new world supra government will be met with overwhelming force and the complete genocide of the enemies of socialism. [60]

This all sounds very threatening, but by 1997 it was also very routine. In 1994, a Canadian journalist named Serge Monast had introduced the conspiracy world to something called "Project Blue Beam" – a multi-stage effort by nefarious forces to produce simulacra, using amazing holographic technology that was no doubt inspired by the holodecks of *Star Trek: The Next Generation*, of everything from alien invasions to the return of Christ, all to subjugate humanity. Monast's vision of humanity's frightening future was actually even more paranoid than Cooper's. The parts were all there though – a new world order, Soviet involvement, and the manipulation of culture (religion, flying saucers, and other important memes) to coerce humanity.[61]

As Cooper moved away from the UFO field and closer to the militia movement, his paranoia became more specifically focused on American politics and government. He believed that the Clinton administration was targeting

---

[60] Cooper, "MAJESTYTWELVE." Given Cooper's ties to the far right militia movement and acceptance of the fraudulent "Protocols of the Elders of Zion" as real, it should have come as no surprise that he would single out Friedman, who is Jewish, and who had for years spoken of the need for humanity to move beyond what he called the "tribalism" of nation states in favour of an "earthling" outlook, which implied the very global government that Cooper feared.

[61] Serge Monast, "Project Blue Beam," *Educate Yourself*, 1994, http://educate-yourself.org/cn/projectbluebeam25jul05.shtml.

him for elimination, using the IRS.[62] His shortwave radio show, *The Hour of the Time*, launched in 1993, was often cited by watchdog groups as a prime example of right-wing extremist radio.[63]

In 2002, in what in hindsight seemed like an inevitable end, Cooper was shot and killed in a confrontation with Sherriff's deputies serving a warrant for his arrest at his home in Arizona. Cooper fired upon the deputies first, and severely wounded one of them in the head.[64] Cooper's fans and followers maintain that this was a political assassination, ordered because he had gotten too close to revealing the "truth" of the September 11, 2001 attacks and their true goal of pushing the US toward a New World Order.[65] His influence has continued, with a nearly hagiographic documentary, *The Hour of Our Time*, appearing

---

[62] Cooper had massive amounts of information on the supposed unconstitutionality of the IRS and the income tax on his website. See Milton William Cooper, "B.A.T.F. / IRS CRIMINAL FRAUD," *Veritas*, September 1995, http://goo.gl/tk3EjC.

[63] The complete run of "The Hour of the Time" is available on-line as MP3 files at "Complete Cooper MP3 Collection," *Hour of the Time*, http://goo.gl/7UBkaI.

[64] "Arizona Militia Figure is Shot to Death," *Los Angeles Times*, 7 November 2001; "Conspiracy Theorist Slain in Police Shootout," *Intelligence Report*, Southern Poverty Law Center, Spring 2002, http://goo.gl/fTWPmy.

[65] See, for example, "William Cooper Murdered By Police?: Too Close to The Truth?" *The Irreverent Buddhist*, 14 January 2009, http://goo.gl/W5gQn9.

on the Internet in the last few years.[66]

What I find most interesting about the whole Cooper saga is the way he would constantly reinvent himself, shaping and re-shaping narratives built largely out of other people's ideas and work. To those coming to UFO studies for the first time, Cooper is still sort of a first step in gaining knowledge of the darkest conspiratorial aspects of the field. When delving into the world of MJ-12, the Krill documents, and John Lear's "theories," Cooper's name inevitably comes up. Despite the fact that he denounced as unintentional misinformation much of what he had said in the late 1980s and early 1990s, he remains a pivotal figure.

The connections between Cooper's work and the other theories and trends which have interested me over the past two decades are fascinating and sometimes surprising. Cooper's political ideas share much with some of the more extreme elements of the seven hills dominionists discussed previously, most significantly the hyper-localism and fear of a numinous "secular humanism" being the greatest threat to the United States and – indeed – the world. Cooper's vision of a shadow government and corporate coverups and conspiracy overlaid with ufological tales also owed a great deal to the work of Gray Barker.

There are also, of course, aspects of atemporality in the work of Cooper and his fellow conspiracy peddlers. Their use of the REX-84 exercises discussed earlier is a prime example. An isolated event, existing in a particular historical context, was stripped of almost all meaning. The plan was one of many such military "thought experiments" devised in American history, the vast majority of which were never carried out. In this case, it was designed to secure

---

[66] *The Hour of Our Time*, Ether Films, Dir. James Jankiewicz, 2000. Available for viewing on-line at http://goo.gl/4DiZBO.

assumedly dangerous dissidents in a time of crisis.

I am not, certainly, dismissing the sinister nature of this type of government activity. For all their good qualities, the western democracies have an unfortunate record of erring on the side of repression at times. While REX-84 provides a valuable cautionary example of why civilian oversight of the military is a good thing, in the hands of Cooper and his kind it became an existential threat. They will invoke REX-84 forever, removing it from its natural context and shaping it into something new – a potent weapon in their war against the "new world order."

Cooper's political conspiracies also demonstrated a nostalgia for an America that never really existed. For many on the far right, there is an assumption that once upon a time their goals of local sovreignty, absolute liberty, and a solid economy based upon barter or specie, was the stone cold norm and reality.

This is a myth.

Tension between the federal, state, and local levels has always existed in the United States. Governments routinely dismissed the notion of absolute, boundless liberty (look no further than the Puritan founders of the New England colonies, or Alexander Hamilton and the Federalist founders). The economy has *always* been tenuous and at least partially dependent on paper money of questionable value. The far right's vision of creating a future that looks like the past is undermined by the imaginary nature of the past they wish to restore.

William Cooper will always remain with me because he was my entree into the world of political paranoia all those years ago. His ideas, and the ideas of those he influenced, serve as a very potent and dangerous reminder that there is nothing new under the sun.

CHAPTER SIX

NEW IDEAS
& NEW MEDIA

The Indigenous Hypothesis put forth here argues that some UFOs are in fact real vehicles. But we're not under siege by anthropomorphic ETs or "goblins from hyperspace": the beings behind the curtain are eminently tangible. They insinuate themselves into our ontological context not to confuse us but to camouflage themselves. The UFO spectacle takes on the flavor of myth because it wants to be discounted. At the same time, knowing that their activities are bound to be seen at least occasionally, the occupants deliberately infuse their appearance with what we might expect of genuine extraterrestrial travelers. It's a formidable disguise – but it can be pierced.[67]

On October 18, 2009, those of us who study and think about The Weird and its implications lost one of the keenest intellects who devoted time to these arcane topics. Mac Tonnies thought and wrote about far more than the paranormal, and his blog, *Posthuman Blues*, was a showcase

---

[67] Mac Tonnies, *Posthuman Blues*, 13 December 2006, http://goo.gl/YDwexg. See also Mac Tonnies, *Posthuman Blues: Dispatches From a World on the Cusp of Terminal Dissolution, Volume I* (Redstar Books, 2012), an edited collection of his blog writing for which I was honored to pen the preface.

for ideas ranging from science and the paranormal to cutting edge design and technology. Though probably most well-known today for his development of the "cryptoterrestrial" hypothesis as a possible explanation for some UFO encounters (to which the quotation above is related), his work ranged far beyond that. His first published work was science fiction, followed by extensive writing on the potential for interplanetary archaeology (of which his *After the Martian Apocalypse* was the culmination).[68]

I never met Mac in person, though we corresponded online semi-regularly via email and Twitter. I admired him greatly for his ideas and the clarity with which he expressed them. Even after a few years, I believe that the cryptoterrestrial idea is at least as possible as the extraterrestrial, not necessarily because of my experiences or physical evidence but because Mac was able to express the possibility of hidden peoples on our planet with such style.[69]

---

[68] Mac Tonnies, *After The Martian Apocalypse: Extraterrestrial Artifacts and the Case for Mars Exploration* (Paraview Pocket Books, 2004).

[69] Mac Tonnies, *The Cryptoterrestrials: A Meditation on Indigenous Humanoids and the Aliens Among Us* (Anomalist Books, 2010). Published after his death, *The Cryptoterrestrials* was a thought-provoking re-imagining of the UFO phenomenon, drawing upon a broad panoply of memes, from the "hollow earth" stories of Richard Shaver in the 1940s to John Keel's ultraterrestrials of the 1970s. The cryptoterrestrial hypothesis (which was really more of a thought experiment, designed as much to raise questions as provide firm answers, by Tonnies' own admission) posited that at least some accounts of alien visitation can be attributed to a non-human species indigenous to the Earth that has adapted to our numerical superiority by developing a surprisingly robust technology.

Not that Mac ever really seemed sold completely on any idea – even his own. This, as well, was something to admire. He sought clues rather than answers and understood that knowledge could come from stories as well as science. Mac was a true skeptic who retained a sense of wonder about the universe, our world, and humanity.

Even today, when looking at something interesting online, I find myself wanting to send Mac the link on Twitter to see what his view is. Sometimes I still do, just in case he's paying attention from beyond, in whatever posthuman state he's achieved.

Mac was unique in the literal sense that there's no one really like him out there in what we call the paranormal "scene." I doubt there ever will be. It seemed fitting for me to begin a discussion of "new ideas" in the paranormal with my recollections of Mac's ideas. I wonder how deeply entwined with the paranormal world he would have remained had he lived. Like many of the most impressive thinkers on the matter, such as Jacques Vallee, he probably would have moved away from the topic after a time. But despite their absence from the field – by choice or through their exit from the mortal realm – thinkers and writers like Vallee and John Keel have continued to cast a lasting presence over these issues. Tonnies will as well.

It's ghosts again, of course. Mac Tonnies and other thinkers have often found themselves labeled a latter day Keel or Vallee. Even when presented with ideas that are largely original, people involved in the paranormal, whether the topic is UFOs, cryptozoology, hauntings, or anything else, seem to be locked into the event horizon of an intellectual comfort zone in which they need to place new ideas within an existing framework. This is an understandable response, of course. It's not terribly useful, however, for pushing a field of inquiry forward.

The problem is that there are few truly new ideas coming out of the UFO field. Endless recitations of the variations on abductions and government conspiracies fill the podcast and broadcast airwaves. The exopolitics movement has taken some of the tropes of the old Contactees and blended them with a pinch of paranoia that brings nothing new to the table (more on them later). Occasionally, there are some interesting remixes of these ideas, such as Tonnies' cryptoterrestrials, but for the most part ufology and related fields seem to be stuck on terminal repeat.

A glance at the topics list for the venerable *Coast to Coast AM* radio show illustrates the current poverty of ideas.[70] As I write this, the most recent show was on "The Cholesterol Myth." Upcoming shows include "Geo-Engineering Threats" and a discussion of the ongoing drone controversy. This show, for many a standard of the paranormal media, is seemingly moving further and further afield from those topics, addressing a wider range of political, social, and economic themes. This is completely understandable, as one can only keep a show going for so long endlessly rerunning generations-old ideas.

And yet...

The notion that *every* episode of *Coast to Coast* during the old Art Bell years was a groundbreaking classic is a bit of a stretch. Bell, who created the show and built a loyal following before he left in 2007, did his share of topical, political, non-paranormal interviews and topics. The interview with the LAPD's Mark Fuhrman (of OJ Simpson

---

[70] *Coast to Coast AM with George Noory*, Premiere Networks, Inc., http://www.coasttocoastam.com/.

trial fame) is a particular incongruous installment.[71] These episodes don't stick in our heads, however, creating this fog of myth; a sense of what "real" *Coast to Coast AM* should be. Like most fans of a show, team, or band, I have a very firm sense of what the best era for *Coast to Coast* was. For me, Art Bell from about 1996 to 1999 was nearly the most entertaining a radio host has ever been.

Not that he or his show was perfect. He fell prey to some of the dangers that all such shows face. It is not difficult to find, within the culture of the paranormal and the constellation of media that has arisen around it, evidence of a desire to find absolute yes or no answers to questions of haunting, extraterrestrial life, cryptozoological specimens, or psychic ability. Art Bell, while a masterful radio host, was never a particular fan of ambiguity. He preferred the easy answers.

For example, on my way into work one morning, I was listening to a recording of Art Bell's *Dreamland* show from 1995. His guest was Glenn Campbell, a longtime researcher of US government activities at the mysterious Area 51 installation. Throughout the interview Campbell emphasized the ambiguity of the Area 51/Dreamland/S-4 narrative, and described it as a blend of conventional military activity and activity which might have had something to do with alien technology. That sounds straightforward, but Campbell was cautious, almost cagey, in presenting any conclusions. Most impressive to me was that Campbell described the Area 51 story as "folklore" and described his role as a researcher as being one of putting together the pieces of a grand narrative. This would, he

---

[71] "Mark Fuhrman interview," *Coast to Coast AM*, 4 September 1997, http://scratchpad.wikia.com/wiki/Coast_to_Coast_AM_-_Index_of_Shows.

asserted, allow him to find consistencies that may one day lead to a kind of truth.

Art Bell, of course, was having none of this ambiguity. His show – his shtick, really – was dependent on sensational information presented as absolute truth. Campbell seemed, in this installment, to rub Bell the wrong way from the very beginning. This uneasiness on Bell's part stemmed mostly from Campbell's reluctance to express any conclusions. The most representative portion of this conversation came during the first hour. Campbell was persisting in his careful, balanced view of Area 51 sightings as being a blend of conventional military craft, unconventional military craft, and genuine unexplained phenomenon.

Bell finally lot his patience with all of this interesting nuance and said something along the lines of, "If I picked you up and threw you into a wall and made you tell me what your view of extraterrestrial visitors was, what would you say?"

Campbell fired back by stating that, "I'd throw you against a wall and explain that I'm following an unfolding mystery." I laughed out loud, disturbing the pedestrian who watched the whole thing while I was stopped at a traffic light. Sadly, Bell's browbeating paid off and before the top of the hour newsbreak, Campbell acknowledged his belief that the visitors were here, but that they were benevolent.

I hit stop on my phone's audio player. I had heard enough. True to form, Art Bell would not go back to the realms of speculative folklore and myth building. He had an answer – space aliens! – that satisfied the demands of his show's format and that was really all he needed. This is, of course, part of the problem with most "paranormal" themed media. Each type of show – I'm focusing on the radio phenomenon, but there are multiple manifestations of paranormal media – carries with it expectations on both sides of the screen or speaker. During the 1990s, Art Bell's shows – *Coast to Coast AM* and *Dreamland* – fulfilled a particular purpose. That purpose was to make money for Art Bell, Chancellor Broadcasting, Premiere Broadcasting, and whatever other entities had a financial stake in the production and distribution of the show, from advertisers to local radio stations. In order to accomplish that goal, Bell developed a formula that made money for most of a decade, even after he left the show. George Noory (among others) took over *Coast to Coast AM*; *Dreamland* spun off to become a vehicle for Whitley Strieber's ideas and products.

This was the general idea – a combination of unscreened calls from the dead of night and interviews with guests who had ideas that ranged from the paranormally "safe" (UFO sighting reports, abduction stories) to the more bizarre, such as "Mel's Hole", in which Mel Waters claimed he had discovered a mysterious bottomless pit in eastern Washington.[72] Drawing upon these disparate threads, Bell wove a tapestry embroidered by paranormal and conspiracy thought, albeit one that was as shallow as it was wide.

There were others, of course. The Paranet Continuum was a weekly radio show that fostered a slightly more skeptical, ambiguous approach than did Art Bell. Jeff Rense's radio show featured many of the same guests as Art Bell and, at its height in the 1990s, was carried on major radio networks. Rense, however, veered further into political conspiracy than did most paranormal themed shows. His guests would not only discuss flying saucers and

---

[72] Brian Dunning, "Falling Into Mel's Hole," *Skeptoid*, 2 June 2009, http://skeptoid.com/episodes/4156. See also Mike Johnston, "Getting to the bottom of Mel's Hole," *Daily Record*, 2 April 2012, http://goo.gl/7gIBkR.

the like, but also the dangers of the New World Order and the coming elimination of freedom throughout the world. Rense's website featured huge volumes of "news" ranging from mainstream stories at CNN to the reptilian ramblings of David Icke and anti-Semitic postings from a variety of far right "pundits."[73]

So while there was a spectrum of voices among paranormal media, a basic pattern emerged in the 1990s. Shows would have guests, callers, and an online presence to back up the whole thing. This has largely been copied in the world of paranormal-themed podcasting in recent years, although the presence of callers has diminished in favor of a dialogue between the host and the guest.[74] In general, this has led to a diffusion of voices across the Internet, even as it has resulted in the consolidation of voices at the corporate mainstream radio level. What they all have in common is that they seem to echo each other and their progenitors from years past.

I submit that Art Bell's popularity, and the impact of the show, had less to do with his skills as host, which were considerable, than the period during which his show was at its height. The mid-to-late 1990s was a time of tremendous ferment in the paranormal world, particularly the UFO

---

[73] A number of commentators have asserted that Rense himself is anti-Semitic based on what he posts at his website. See, for example, Paul Kimball, "Introduction," *The Rense Watch*, 26 May 2005, http://goo.gl/ZnohnU.

[74] One of the first, and best, of these podcasts was *Binnall of America*, created in 2005 by Tim Binnall, a young Syracuse communications graduate from Massachusetts with an interest in Fortean subjects. As of 2013, the program remains active, with a loyal following, having outlasted myriad other podcasts that have come and gone since it began. www.binnallofamerica.com.

field, and Bell took advantage of it all, riding the zeitgeist to ever-increasing ratings. Roswell was *interesting* – as its fiftieth anniversary approached, there were government investigations and countless new books emerging. *The X-Files* made the paranormal very nearly sexy. Most of all, the Internet, with its burgeoning World Wide Web and more traditional Usenet service, was bringing paranormal devotees together in ways which were undreamt of a decade before. Art Bell's shows were the culmination of these factors and events rather than their impetus.

I have often been struck by how much of the real intellectual work in the realm of the paranormal is done by those who are not the huge names. People like Stanton Friedman have contributed much, but they have also been trading on work which was initiated decades ago, making appearances, earning money and – more often than we like to admit, no matter how much we might enjoy listening to them – contributing nothing new.

I've often learned more, and had my perceptions *really* challenged, by listening to podcasts like *Radio Misterioso* than I have by listening to *Coast to Coast AM* or *Dreamland*.[75] In print, increasingly, those popularly published paranormal books (and there seem to be fewer of them every year as publishing and public tastes shift) are merely the primary sources for an investigation of the cultural phenomenon of "paranormal belief and marketing." The indie publishing insurgence has produced a massive number of new books that are worth a look, but such prodigious output threatens to veer into information overload. When I listen to a show,

---

[75] Radio Misterioso is a weekly (for the most part) on-line radio program hosted by Los Angeles-based author and researcher Greg Bishop, who was also one of the founders of the *Excluded Middle* magazine in the 1990s. www.radiomisterioso.com.

pick up a book, or land on a website, I have one request of the creators (one I hope to fulfill in my own work). Don't tell me your answers, and don't just rehash the same old ideas and stories. Present me with questions, and encourage new ways of thinking. Inspire me to delve further into those weird, dark intersections between belief and science, thought and matter, real and unreal, rational and non-rational.

In other words, be like Mac Tonnies.

CHAPTER SEVEN

THE TYRANNY OF LANGUAGE & PLACE

In the summer of 2012, while I was deeply immersed in the writing of my book *Extraterrestrials and the American Zeitgeist*, I posted the following note on my blog, partly as a progress update, and partly as a form of on-line self-reflection:

> And, of course, adding in the section about Billy Meier, the Swiss Contactee whose story spans decades. Whole lot of information to sort through there, but I think I have an approach that's narrow enough that it doesn't become the Billy Meier chapter (it's in with the 1970s stuff). One of the biggest issues with the Meier material is that the original translations of the 1970s notes are pretty heavily edited (editor Wendelle Stevens removed inflammatory statements about religion and politics. I mean, what's the *point*? Oh, and I think I met Stevens once, back in '96 at a UFO slideshow in a hotel conference room. Not sure though...). Still, I think it works for my overall approach and, besides, a book about Contactees without Billy Meier

doesn't really work...[76]

This passage, from Wendelle Stevens's commentary on one of Meier's transmissions, sums up his attitude well:

> Some of those comments are damaging to certain personalities, and even libelous under our laws, and so we have taken exception to Quetzal's demand and have edited and deleted as we considered appropriate. Those deletions are the gaps in the sentence numbering sequence for each of the Pleiadian speakers shown here in our version of the contact message from the Pleiades. Another reason for some of the larger gaps in the numbering sequence, is our deletion of unkind references to our various religions and beliefs, and to our political systems, petty as they may seem to the extraterrestrials. These systems are ours, and we live here, and in our free right to choose, we make the choices which may seem expedient to us.[77]

---

[76] Aaron J. Gulyas, "Hack and Slash," *History, Teaching and the Strange*, 12 July 2012, http://goo.gl/K8pSr2. Billy Meier is a citizen of Switzerland who has been the source of many UFO photographs, claims of personal contact, and prophecies since the 1960s. He is considered by the majority of UFO researchers, and virtually all skeptics, to be a fraud.

[77] Wendelle Stevens, *Message from the Pleiades, Volume 1* (UFO Photo Archives, 1988), 265.

Stevens notes that the decision to perform these edits was taken over the desires and instructions of "Quetzal," one of Meier's extraterrestrial contacts. There are now a few different extant sources for translation of the Meier statements that have an "official" blessing from the source. The Stevens work, however, was the first exposure many in the English-speaking world had to the Meier story and, thus, the question of reliability in the translations and (especially) the question of what was left out of the Pleideans' messages looms large.

Or, to be more precise, they might have loomed large if Meier's photographs and claims had not been debunked. Forget about that for now, though. As you have, hopefully, seen throughout these essays, the notion of determining literal truth or falsehood, while often necessary, is not nearly as much fun as performing bizarre thought experiments based on these stories, whether half-true, partially-true, or not true at all.

While it was a point I discussed briefly in *Extraterrestrials and the American Zeitgeist*, until recently I had forgotten mentioning it on my blog. I think one of the quandaries I ran into while writing the book – about Stevens' translation and editing of Meier's contact notes (published in several volumes as *Message from the Pleiades*) – speaks to a broader point about place and language in the study of flying saucers, UFOs, and other anomalous things.

My research, writings, academic conference presentations, and books have all been relentlessly American. The exceptions have been few and far between. Inevitably that means some important things may get lost in translation when I take a look at stories from non-American locales.

For example, Elizabeth Klarer is a South African Contactee whose story fits in nicely with work on Contactee romance.[78] The tales of Antonio Villas Boas and Billy Meier are crucial for gaining an understanding of the wide range of Contact experiences.[79] But these cases are outliers, not just in my work but I believe in the Anglophone iteration of the field's literature in general. Even when they are discussed it is at a fairly distant remove.

Let us, for a moment, set aside Klarer's case. She wrote her own words, in English, so she's a bit different. My understanding (like most other American researchers) of the Villas Boas encounter with the beautiful and strange red-headed woman comes from Coral and Jim Lorenzen's *Flying Saucer Occupants*, which contains a translation of the report by Olavo Fontes and Joao Martins.[80] I've never read the original report in Portuguese, because I don't read Portuguese. I'm relying on a filtered, translated account, much like I had to do

---

[78] Elizabeth Klarer, *Beyond the Light Barrier: The Autobiography of Elizabeth Klarer* (Howard Timmins, 1980). Klarer claimed to have been contacted by extraterrestrials between 1954 and 1963. She was one of the first women to claim a sexual relationship with an extraterrestrial.

[79] Aaron John Gulyas, *Extraterrestrials and the American Zeitgeist: Alien Contact Tales Since the 1950s* (McFarland, 2013), 210 – 213. Antonio Villas Boas was a Brazilian farmer who claimed to have been abducted by extraterrestrials in 1957. His story was among the first alien abduction accounts to receive widespread attention.

[80] Coral Lorenzen and James Lorenzen, *Flying Saucer Occupants* (Signet, 1967), 42-72.

with the Meier material.

Now, for someone who is primarily concerned with physical evidence this is a not necessarily a huge concern. A scorch-mark on the ground, radiation burns on a witness, or video footage of mysterious lights in the sky are largely, though not always entirely, independent of the vagaries of language. Personal accounts, though, are a different matter. The expertise of the translator, and their understanding of the peculiarities of particular idioms or dialects, plays a crucial role in conveying the weightier messages and delicate nuances of the stories. In the case of Villas Boas or Meier, there may certainly be shades of meaning that do not come across well to readers in a different time or place.

Added to this, potentially, is the question of translation between any extraterrestrial visitors – or ghosts, or denizens of hidden civilizations... let's not limit ourselves – and witnesses or experiencers that they may encounter. Many Contactees claimed that their communications with the Space Brothers and Sisters were psychic or telepathic in nature.[81] This would

---

[81] Canadian Contactee Wilbert Smith described communication with aliens as follows: "The mental images of the person wishing to transmit are picked up electrically amplified and modulated into a tensor beam, which is directed to the person to whom the transmission is addressed, and within whose brain the mental images are recreated. The transmissions are therefore very precise, and independent of language. I have had some experience with these transmissions myself and can say that they are like nothing within the conventional experiences of earth people." Wilbert Smith, "Canadian Program Director Discusses Communication With Aliens," *Presidential UFO*, 1961, Radio, http://goo.gl/HTmyjl.

certainly alleviate some of the concerns about translation and language problems.

It is more likely, however, that whatever non-human intelligent life we find will communicate in some way that we cannot comprehend. In fact – and this is a salient point with regard to Contactees especially – our conception of "intelligence" (even when discussing potential extraterrestrials) is irrevocably grounded in an anthropocentric framework. In other words, we expect non-humans to be just like humans, only from somewhere else.

This is most evident with the Contactees, but even those who discuss the "Greys" often ascribe motivations and activities, whether positive or negative, that are recognizably human Even the general structure of described alien life forms – head, torso, limbs – is humanoid. This is not a novel idea, but it bears repeating that all of our knowledge of life and intelligence is based on an understanding that is limited to one planet out of the entire universe. Any visitors we encounter are likely to be unrecognizable to us as *life*, much less as intelligent life.

If we were to encounter a form of intelligent life from beyond our planet, how would we discuss it? Do our human languages have the ability to describe what we would see, let alone allow us to communicate with these otherworldly beings? If nothing else, the various theories that use time travel, inter-dimensional beings, or a previously hidden Earth-based humanoid species as an explanation for "extraterrestrial" experiences provide a way to do at least a partial end run around the issue of language and cultural barriers.

We are prisoners of words. Even inside the solitude of

our own minds, our thoughts take the form of language. If we imagine a flower, the word "flower" is floating around in our headspace. On Earth, language and complex communication are signifiers that separate humans from other animals. What might be the line of demarcation on other worlds? What denotes intelligence on far-off worlds? I tried, as I wrote this chapter, to imagine an intelligent culture that had no language, to which the very concept of language – verbal or written, or even gestural – is foreign. I am unable to do so, for I find that I need my own words to describe their lack of words.[82]

A popular analogy, among those who fear the coming of the space beings, is to compare us to the Inca and the aliens to Pizzaro. While this may be a useful way to envisage a technological gap between humanity and those who may come from the stars, Pizzaro and the Inca were both human. Though the differences between our human cultures may seem significant, in comparison to the potential differences between humans and intelligent nonhumans from other planets, Pizzaro and the Inca were virtually identical.

The members of the human race are tethered both to each other and, for the moment, to the planet. We may be able to escape this little blue marble, but we will never truly escape our humanity. For all our bold talk of post-humanism, the very concept is grounded in humanity. The machines which we would morph into would be our own creations – even if the machines eventually became

---

[82] For an excellent discussion of language, communication and how it might relate to an advanced non-human intelligence, see Kimball, *The Other Side of Truth*, pp. 10 – 31.

self-replicating and self-aware, their origin would still lie with humans.

The concepts of language and culture bind us together as humans as much as biology. While someday we will visit other planets, *place* will remain important. It certainly looms large in UFO literature. Well-known anomalous events are often categorized and described by their location. Roswell, Phoenix, Kecksburg, Malmstrom, Aztec, Shag Harbour, Rendlesham – these are all places one can visit.

Place is crucial, for example, in the Contactee memoir of Elizabeth Klarer, *Beyond the Light Barrier*. This is a story that is intensely bound up in place – in her case, South Africa in the 1950s. Leaving aside the alien contact aspects of her story, because in general I find that this actually makes the story more compelling, Klarer's tale is that of a fairly privileged white woman living through a time of wrenching transition to the postcolonial era.[83]

While Klarer's story originated in the 1950s (and summaries of it appeared in flying saucer journals of the time), her book is a work of the 1970s – of an age when Apartheid faced the challenges of international condemnation and internal violence and chaos. The book is full of references to a coming race war, along with overtones of white supremacy. It is a work that only could have emerged from that place at that time and is a fine example of the role that place plays in our lives and our stories. Even if we leave our village, nation, or planet, we will still be in some *place* – and that place will shape

---

[83] Klarer, *Beyond the Light Barrier*. See also Elizabeth Klarer, "Live Speech of Her UFO Experiences," *YouTube*, http://youtu.be/0OTqvcDhplU.

our stories.

I used the word "tyranny" in the title of this chapter because we cannot, for the moment, escape it. Someday, perhaps, we will be able to do so. When that day comes, if we can transcend the need for language, then we will truly be post-humans. The future of humanity is not necessarily an endless parade of Google Glass-like digital appendages hanging off of us. Rather, I think to be beyond human we will have to learn to thrive without fundamental things like language.

At that point, perhaps the aliens will make more sense. Perhaps – and, again, this is nothing I can *prove*, but I enjoy thinking about it – the "aliens" are post-language humans. They (or is it *we*) may retain a sort of vestigial notion of what language is and what it is for, which allows them (or is it *us*) to communicate in ways that are recognizable, if odd and slightly wrong, at least to us.

My anthropologist friends and colleagues who may read this will, by this point, have abandoned most, if not all, hope for my sanity and powers of rational thinking. They may have a point. One could argue that to abandon language would be devolution rather than evolution. Language, after all, was a significant, defining milestone in human development. But so was domesticating the horse, until we eventually invented the automobile.

Someday we will not need language, at least not as we currently understand it. I have a feeling that we will find this terrifying and wrong. After a few millennia of language-less humanity, some heretics will seek out what they had lost. They will come back in time, and talk to twentieth century humanity, all to relearn the ancient mystery of having a conversation.

CHAPTER EIGHT

EXOPOLITICS

In my continuing quest to find new angles from which to approach the various bits of cultural debris that surrounds the paranormal, I've always had trouble getting a good grip on exopolitics (or perhaps it should be "exopolitics," as one should always place silly neologisms within sarcastic quotation marks), the movement within ufology that began in the early 2000s and has come to dominate the subculture in the decade since.[84]

I have neither the time nor the patience to undertake a full-on explanation of the phenomenon (although I do discuss the parallels between it and traditional Contactee movements in *Extraterrestrials and the American Zeitgeist*). But,

---

[84] The de facto founders of the movement are Alfred Webre and Michael Salla. For Webre, see www.exopolitics.com, and his book *Exopolitics: Politics, Government, and Law in the Universe* (2005). Salla has a Ph.D in Government from the University of Queensland, Australia, and an M.A. in Philosophy from the University of Melbourne. The two fell out in early 2011 over claims made by Andrew Basiago that were supported by Webre but disputed by Salla in which Basiago stated he had been to Mars. Salla countered that Basiago was a "mind control victim" who had been, "tasked to manipulate and handle Webre." See Michael Salla, "Statement on Alfred Webre and his role in Exopolitics," *Exopolitics*, 27 January 2011, http://exopolitics.org/Exo-Comment-98.htm. For more information, see Salla's website at www.exopolitics.org, and his book *Exopolitics: Political Implications of Extraterrestrial Presence* (Dandelion Books, 2004).

in brief, exopolitics (I'll forgo the quotation marks – I'm feeling generous) positions itself as a new branch of political science that, in the words of arch-exopolitician Michael Salla, deals with, "the study of the key individuals, political institutions and processes associated with extraterrestrial life."[85]

Oh dear. Where to begin?

I guess I'll start with the phrase "extraterrestrial life," for it is a given in the world of exopolitics that such life exists. I don't have a problem with that assumption. As I've discussed, I think it's scientifically, theologically, rationally, and non-rationally probable that non-human intelligences exist, and that some of them may, in fact, not be from Earth. This is, of course, the broadest definition of "extraterrestrial." The exopolitics movement, however, uses an extremely narrow definition of "extraterrestrial." On Salla's website, for example, there is a collection of links entitled "Initiatives." The links all lead to an online petition site where people can express their support for things like, "Sign Petition for US Senate Inquiry into Ike's ET Meeting" and the "Hawaii Declaration on Peaceful Relations with Extraterrestrial Civilizations."

One in particular that caught my eye was entitled "We need your consent." This differed a bit from other items like "Galactic Freedom Day Declaration." Clicking through I found what purported to be a telepathic transmission from humanity's "family from the stars." Who is this family? Here's their claim:

> We are those who watch over you in your
> hours of need and whisper to you that all will
> be well. We inspire and assist your creations
> from the realms of the unseen and yet we are as

> real as you, in every way we are you. We are
> just a little more spiritually advanced,
> technologically and socially superior because
> we have already traveled this road you now
> walk upon.[86]

This sounds familiar, I thought to myself. Getting up and walking to my bookshelf of paranormal shame, I grabbed a couple books and flipped through them. These books, *Project: Earth Evacuation* and *Ashtar: A Tribute* were "compiled" by a woman calling herself Tuella in the 1980s.[87] The message is largely the same – intergalactic friends who were once as horrible as we are now surround humanity. They got better, we still haven't, and we need their help. This, of course, is where the "consent" part comes in.

You see, the Space Buddies cannot help us without our request of their support and intervention. This is, of course, couched in talk of free will, because free will is paramount – just as in *Star Trek*, which some in the paranormal field apparently thought was a documentary, protagonists must abide by the Prime Directive unless the plot dictates otherwise. The Prime Directive, of course, is that the advanced and benevolent (except when it's not) United Federation of Planets cannot interfere in the development of lesser civilizations (except when it does). It works the same way with our Space Buddies, as noted in the "We Need Your Consent" petition:

---

[86] "We Need Your Consent," *Petition Online*, http://goo.gl/Xb5qMW.

[87] Tuella, *Project: World Evacuation by the Ashtar Command* (Guardian Action Publications, 1987); Tuella, *Ashtar: A Tribute* (Guardian Action Publications, 1987).

Do you want war? Poverty? Illness? Violence and suffering? Or do you want achievement, the restoring of nature, new energies and Earth friendly technologies? Do you want a 30 year period of peace and balanced ideas founded within the innate integrity of humanity? Do you want us, your star neighbors and friends, to help you mitigate the most destructive of the climatic and earth movements and to show you, to give to you and your world, new models and systems based upon harmonious principles that align the goals of citizens with the needs of the planet herself? Do you wish to stabilize your ideas and world to enter in divine grace this new era of peace and happiness? We beseech you to ask for our help. We must have your consent; we will by our own laws force nothing, absolutely nothing upon you and your world.[88]

Of course, this makes perfect sense. If I see my son playing next to a fire, getting closer and closer to the flames, I can't really do anything about it unless he makes some explicit indication that he wants my help. What kind of father would I be if I forced my will upon him, getting him away from the fire, helping him whether he wanted to be helped or not?

Child Protective Services, a judge, a jury, and my wife might, however, have very different opinions of my well-meaning respect for my son's free will. This is where the parent/child (or advanced/primitive) model for our alleged relationship with extraterrestrials as presented by the exopolitics movement falls apart. In the spirit of Captain

---

[88] "We Need Your Consent," Ibid.

James T. Kirk, who regularly contravened the Prime Directive in *Star Trek*, I do not believe that standing idly by while the less-capable destroy themselves is ethical behavior.

And yet appears that the aliens do.

The inappropriate and inconsistent parent-child analogy is far from the only thing that annoys me about the exopolitics movement. There is also a profound and frustrating naïveté that overrides most of their discussions. The blithe acceptance of any story, from any person, that fits with any of their previously held beliefs, often approaches ludicrous extremes. One example is a posting from a few years ago entitled "First Anniversary of Declaration to end secret extraterrestrial agreements" (August 7, 2009):

> Exactly one year ago a consortium of citizen organizations authorized a Declaration to end what were claimed to be secret official agreements concerning extraterrestrial life. Based on first hand testimonies by a number of whistleblowers and civilian contractors, the Galactic Freedom Day Declaration asserts that agreements concerning extraterrestrial life have been secretly entered into by a number of government authorized agencies, departments and corporations. In some cases, these agreements involve representatives of advanced extraterrestrial civilizations whose existence has not been disclosed to the general public. On 08/08/08 individuals and citizen organizations around the world collectively joined in events calling for exposing and ending such agreements. A consortium of citizen organizations from Hawaii, USA, Canada,

Britain, Spain, South Africa, and Hong Kong formally sponsored the Declaration and launched an online petition which currently has over 2000 signatures. The Declaration affirms a number of citizen rights with regard to extraterrestrial life. These include the "natural right of all citizens to have safe and open contact with extraterrestrial visitors, and to engage in non-official diplomacy." If extraterrestrial civilizations are visiting Earth, the natural right of private citizens to interact with such visitors is clearly an important issue requiring some kind of legislative recognition.[89]

Their petition called for an end to "what were claimed to be" secret agreements. There was no actual fact presented here (or in any exopolitics document). A key phrase, however, comes in the second paragraph: "natural right of all citizens to have safe and open contact with extraterrestrial visitors, and to engage in non-official diplomacy." Is there such a thing as non-official diplomacy? Dictionary.com defines the word "diplomacy" as:

1. the conduct by government officials of negotiations and other relations between nations.

2. the art or science of conducting such negotiations.

3. skill in managing negotiations, handling people, etc., so that there is little or no ill will; tact: Seating one's dinner guests often calls for

---

[89] Michael Salla, "First Anniversary of Declaration to end secret extraterrestrial agreements," *Honolulu Exopolitics Examiner*, 7 August 2009, http://goo.gl/hhzwMS.

considerable diplomacy.[90]

At best, I can see definition 3 fitting a "non-governmental" use of the term. To use a terrestrial example, if I talk to someone from Russia, *I'm talking to someone from Russia* – I'm not engaging in any kind of diplomacy. Of course the exopolitics crowd would shift focus back onto the question of whether or not the public should be made aware of these alleged visitors. That's actually a really good question – but is it the best question?

One camp answers "yes!" mostly because some (but not all) "whistleblowers" have told them that the visitors are friendly, part of a galactic federation here for our own good. Others say "no!" because they fear the visitors are demons (or, as Russ Dizdar calls them, *homo satanas*) – or, if not demons, then certainly evil entities very much akin to the Lear/Cooper/Krill abduction and mutilation fantasias of the 80s and 90s.

Both of these answers assume that the visitors are aliens from another planet (or spiritual dimension in the case of the "Christian" interpretations of the phenomenon). It never seems to occur to either the exopolitics / spacebuddy crowd, or the para-evangelical fringe, that they aren't dealing with what they think they are. Of course, like all of us, to one degree or another, they may simply be willfully avoiding looking at information or ideas that contradict the notions that are their bread and butter.

In the end, as we look at the many, many facets of these phenomena and examine reports and findings from all sides, rather than simply those with which we happen to agree, we might find the question is not whether or not we should be allowed to talk to the visitors and engage in diplomacy with them, but rather whether the concept of

[90] "Diplomacy," *Dictionary.com*, http://goo.gl/uPT6iu.

"diplomacy" makes sense in such a context. It might be akin to opening diplomatic discussions with a tornado or thunderstorm; it might be as futile as politely asking the mosquitoes to stop biting us.

Whatever it is, it won't be what anybody expects. The phenomenon will make sure of that – whatever it or they may represent seems to take delight in confounding our expectations.

But what if all the claims of the exopolitics enthusiasts *were* true? What kind of world would that be? Analysis of the exopolitics phenomenon has led me to the conclusion that it represents, more than anything, Contacteeism viewed through a lens of post-Watergate, post-Church Committee cynicism and paranoia.[91] As a thought experiment, however, the exopolitics movement becomes more interesting.

The exopolitics crowd, for example, was very excited by the 2008 election of Barack Obama. As an American of mixed racial parentage who promised openness, transparency, and change, he seemed (at least to exopolitics enthusiasts) like the ideal politician to reveal the "truth" about the extraterrestrial presence to the world. John

---

[91] The "Church Committee" was a US Senate committee convened in 1975 to investigate claims of abuse on the part of federal intelligence and law enforcement agencies. Its findings included evidence of everything from illegal wiretapping to CIA assassination plots, and has provided ample fuel for conspiratorial paranoia ever since, based on the premise that if this is what we *knew* the government was up to, what was still secret? See: Senate Select Committee to Study Governmental Operations With Respect To Intelligence Activities, "Final Report of the Select Committee to Study Governmental Operations With Respect to Intelligence Activities," 94th Congress, 2nd Session, No. 94-755 (1976), available on-line at: http://goo.gl/bxzXHw.

Podesta, a former Clinton administration Chief of Staff who managed the Obama transition team after the 2008 election, was a known fan of *The X-Files*, which was taken as another sign that pointed to Obama being the man who would finally end the decades-long cover-up, as was the appointment by Obama of Podesta's predecessor as Clinton's Chief of Staff, Leon Panetta, as the Director of the CIA.[92]

So let's imagine an alternate universe where Obama finally acknowledged the extraterrestrial presence amongst us – the "disclosure" moment for which the exopolitics movement has been waiting. In this world, a few days after his inauguration Obama addressed the world at the United Nations. He revealed the long association between the United States and extraterrestrial polities. He discussed the history of the cover-up and the vast array of fantastic technology the United States and other major powers such as the Russians, the British, the French, and the Chinese perhaps, have been hoarding. It's a masterful speech – Obama is a fine orator – but the consequences of it are a bit out of line with what the exopolitics crowd expects.

Far from uniting the American people and the world, the acknowledgement of extraterrestrial life further divides them. The old, clichéd fear that religious Americans would be unable to cope with the knowledge that extraterrestrial life exists proves, mostly, unfounded. The Roman Catholic

---

[92] Michael Salla, "Obama's choice of CIA Director signals renewed effort to disclose CIA X-Files," *Exopolitics.com*, 7 January 2009, http://goo.gl/ITRtkl. Salla predicted that, "The choice of Panetta as CIA Director signals that the Obama administration is also interested in the declassification of files concerning UFOs. Panetta will likely spearhead efforts by the Obama administration to pressure the CIA to release its deepest held secrets – the CIA's X-Files." Alas, it hasn't quite worked out that way.

Church, mainline Protestant denominations, Jewish authorities, and leading Islamic scholars quickly find ample precedent for incorporating this knowledge into their worldview. Fundamentalist Protestants are mostly concerned with the mission opportunities and how to market their mega-churches to aliens. No, the division is political.

Republican leaders quickly pounce on the President's speech, pointing out that he spent more time blaming Republican administrations for the cover-up than accepting responsibility for the culpability of Democratic administrations. Citizens in the nation's already suffering industrial areas worry about the impact of ET technology on their jobs. Proponents of more stringent immigration restriction have an entirely new set of concerns. Right and Left wing journalists and commentators speculate on the timing of the announcement. Was the new President simply trying to distract attention from the looming fiscal crisis? Meanwhile, around the globe world leaders not in the know express outrage.

In short, I honestly don't think a stunning announcement about the existence not only of extraterrestrials but of our nation's decades-long cover-up of them will have as drastic a change on our lives as some think. Faith in our government and our religious institutions will not be undermined (at least, not undermined any more than their own actions have often caused them to be). Political bickering will not cease. Our rapid technological advancement is already taking us into uncharted territory.

Aliens may, in fact, prove to be anticlimactic. Besides, sooner or later some enterprising computer whiz will create an "App" to communicate with our space buddies via your iPad, and the resulting barrage of texts from drunken college kids will convince them that there's no hope for us.

It's all a moot point, really. The exopolitics crowd has never produced a scintilla of evidence for our space buddies that I find even remotely compelling. Their insistence on anthropomorphizing extraterrestrials is frustrating and their politics are naïve. On the other hand, I see the field's utility as a jumping off point for speculation and examination of our own, terrestrial political systems, which are bizarre and out-of-touch enough without bringing Space People into the picture.

CHAPTER NINE
BREAKING ROSWELL

The Roswell incident represents a fascinating example of the depth to which some aspects of the UFO culture have penetrated the wider popular culture. From the teen drama *Roswell* to episodes of *Star Trek: Deep Space Nine* and *Futurama*, Roswell has shown up in a wide variety of places on television, for example. But it is an event about which I am deeply, fiercely conflicted.

Wikipedia provides a good summation of where things stand with the case almost seventy years after it happened, and almost forty years after Stanton Friedman "rediscovered" it:

> The Roswell UFO incident took place in the U.S. in 1947, when an airborne object crashed on a ranch near Roswell, New Mexico, in June or July, 1947. Explanations of what took place are based on both official and unofficial communications. Although the crash is attributed to a U.S. military surveillance balloon by the U.S. government, the most famous explanation of what occurred is that the object was a spacecraft containing extraterrestrial life. Since the late 1970s, the Roswell incident has been the subject of much controversy, and conspiracy theories have arisen about the event. The United States Armed Forces maintains that what was recovered near Roswell was debris from the crash of an experimental high-altitude

surveillance balloon belonging to what was then a classified (top secret) program named Mogul. In contrast, many UFO proponents maintain that an alien craft was found, its occupants were captured, and that the military engaged in a massive cover-up. The Roswell incident has turned into a widely known pop culture phenomenon, making the name "Roswell" synonymous with UFOs. Roswell has become the most publicized of all alleged UFO incidents.[93]

The story of the Roswell crash and supposed cover-up emerged in its modern form in the 1980s, and reached a zenith with its fiftieth anniversary in 1997.[94] Jerome Clark, writing in the March, 1991 issue of *Fate* magazine, traced the history of the topic in ufological circles:

> The earliest printed reference I can find to the Roswell event in this literature is in 1966, in Frank Edwards' *Flying Saucers – Serious Business.* The only other reference appears the next year, in Ted Bloecher's *Report on the UFO Wave of*

---

[93] "Roswell UFO Incident," *Wikipedia*, http://goo.gl/lZEzkL.

[94] Charles Berlitz and William L. Moore, *The Roswell Incident* (Berkely Books, 1980). This was the first book on the Roswell incident, with research conducted by Moore and his partner Stanton Friedman in the mid to late 1970s (Friedman was not credited as an author). Friedman, who had been lecturing about UFOs more or less full time since the late 1960s, would become known as the "Father of Roswell," and has spent the past three decades largely focused on the research and promotion of that one case; see *Stanton T. Friedman is Real*, dir. Paul Kimball, DVD, Redstar Films, 2002, available on-line at http://goo.gl/Xd5auj.

1947, where it is dealt with in three paragraphs under the heading, "Hoaxes and Mistakes." Neither treatment (either Edward's positive one or Bloecher's negative one) had any impact; there are no further references to Roswell in the literature. I have been interested in UFOs since 1957. Until a few years ago I had scarcely heard of it, for the simple reason that it was never talked about.[95]

Crucially, Roswell was not just absent from the earliest UFO literature; tales of crashed saucers and the presence of occupants were largely dismissed by serious researchers as hoaxes and cons.[96] Organizations like NICAP treated most discussion of UFO occupants with skepticism, not wanting to be lumped together with anything even remotely resembling Contactee claims. Until the advent of the abduction phenomenon with all of its familiar trappings,

---

[95] Jerome Clark, "Footnote to Roswell," *Fate Magazine*, March 1991, http://www.fatemag.com/ufos/footnote-to-roswell/.

[96] This antipathy has a great deal to do with the publication by *Variety Magazine* columnist Frank Scully in 1950 of the first crashed flying saucer book, about the alleged "Aztec incident" in northern New Mexico. The "case" was quickly revealed to be a hoax created by two conmen, Silas Newton and Leo Gebauer, who were trying to use it to entice people to buy into their fraudulent oil exploration scheme, which they claimed had access to alien technology. For the original story, see Frank Scully, *Behind the Flying Saucers* (Harry Holt & Co., 1950); for the definitive expose, see J. P. Cahn, "The Flying Saucers and the Mysterious Little Men," *True*, September 1952, 17 – 19, 102 – 112, available on-line at http://goo.gl/uJe1lX, and Cahn, "Flying Saucer Swindlers," *True*, August 1956, 36 – 37, 69 – 71, available on-line at http://goo.gl/arjzkc.

with the Betty and Barney Hill incident being considered the key starting point for that narrative, non-humanoid occupants of supposed outer space craft tended to be fairly diverse, with figures ranging from hairy dwarves to beautiful if strange-looking women.[97]

One example of this is a handy chart in the back of *Flying Saucer Occupants*, a 1967 book by APRO heads Coral and James Lorenzen. It lists a wide variety of saucer crewmembers including:

1. Small monster
2. Large monster
3. Small humanoid
4. Large humanoid
5. Small robot
6. Large robot

These creatures were also categorized by the type of craft sighted, the type of clothing they had ("none," "diving suit," "diving helmet," "ordinary," or "unusual"), and the shape and size of the creatures' eyes.[98] While one could certainly characterize the now-familiar Greys as non-clothing wearing small monsters with large black eyes, such

---

[97] For a skeptical view of the Hill abduction case, see *Cosmos*, "Encyclopaedia Galactica," PBS, 14 December 1980, hosted by Carl Sagan. The episode is available on-line at http://youtu.be/5DgWOlqa-iQ. For the "believer" point of view, see Stanton T. Friedman and Kathleen Marden, *Captured! The Betty and Barney Hill UFO Experience: The True Story of the World's First Documented Alien Abduction* (New Page Books, 2007).

[98] Coral Lorenzen and James Lorenzen, Ibid., 208.

creatures were just one of a menagerie of saucer occupants.[99]

Despite some decline in attention in recent years (as with most things ufological), Roswell has remained a vital component of the UFO scene. As an historian whose work is focused on American culture, the Roswell phenomenon is too significant to ignore. While I have not read every one of the thousands of pages and hundreds of thousands of words expended on the subject in the past few generations, I am familiar with the saga, particularly its cultural aspects. Rather than an in depth critique of the Roswell master-narrative, what follows is a brief précis of the larger shapes of the narrative that I find particularly interesting.

While fascinating as a cultural phenomenon, within the UFO subculture itself Roswell has warped the study of what used to be called flying saucers, conflating the topic with a variety of tangentially related political conspiracy theories.

The UFO world, beginning in the 1980s, began to center around Roswell in a way that it hadn't really ever centered on anything before. Roswell came to dominate the discussion of UFOs to such a degree that to the public, Roswell was the dawn of the age of the flying saucers in 1947, not Kenneth Arnold's sighting that happened a couple of weeks earlier, and which launched a wave of media attention at the time.

I feel fairly strongly about this. I hate how Roswell pushed (and, even today, continues to push) far more interesting events below the attention threshold. I think the Rendlesham case or the Cash-Landrum incident are all

---

[99] The archetypal image of the "grey alien" was first popularized by Whitley Strieber in his book *Communion: A True Story* (Avon, 1987).

much more worthy of the amount of attention Roswell has received from the non-paranormal media.[100] Culturally, I will always believe that the Contactees are more significant to understanding the landscape of post-War America than Roswell, or any dozen other crash-retrieval stories. Roswell – or more accurately, the attention Roswell has received – has eclipsed the broader array of saucerology.

If there were something definitive at the heart of the Roswell mythology this eclipsing might be justified. But there really isn't. Despite the thousands of pages that have been written about Roswell, there has been no definitive "truth" found.

Is whatever happened at Roswell interesting?

Undoubtedly.

Is it important?

Perhaps.

Is it the primary event in the history of The Weird?

Probably not.

But – and this is crucial, if annoying – most people identify the UFO mystery with Roswell. Particularly fascinating to me is that the "downed alien craft confiscated by government" explanation for what happened (and, clearly, *something* happened that July day in 1947) has become so utterly accepted within and without the UFO

---

[100] The Rendlesham Forest incident is the name given to a series of reported sightings by USAF personnel of unexplained lights and the alleged landing of a craft or multiple craft of unknown origin in Rendlesham Forest, Suffolk, England, in late December 1980. See David Clarke, "The Rendlesham Files," *Dr. David Clarke*, http://goo.gl/5fM4Yg. The Cash-Landrum Incident was a reported UFO sighting from the United States in 1980, which the witnesses insisted was responsible for damage to their health. See John F. Schuessler, *The Cash-Landrum UFO Incident* (Geo Graphics, 1998).

community. One demonstration of the standard story's widespread acceptance is that any explanation that differs is generally labeled an "alternative" Roswell theory. Generally, these alternative theories are dismissed out of hand by those within the UFO field (especially those who have a vested interest in the standard narrative being the *only* narrative), and almost entirely ignored by those outside the UFO field.[101]

A bit of an aside – in May, 2013, the exopolitics movement (see the previous chapter), in the person of Stephen Bassett, staged the "Citizens' Hearing on Disclosure." This event was basically a ramped-up iteration of the numerous attempts at hearings and press conferences people like Bassett and Steven Greer have been promoting for the past twenty years, all of which inevitably tie back to the "space alien crash" mythos of Roswell. What made the "Citizens Hearing" a bit different was the use of a "committee" made up of retired members of the US Congress who were paid to hear "testimony" from UFO witnesses and researchers, which the organizers hoped would lend a veneer of credibility to what was, at its heart, just another flying saucer carny sideshow.[102]

Key to the narrative of this hearing, and to the exopolitics movement in general, is the notion that nefarious forces within Western governments have hidden technology from crashed Roswell craft, using it for their

---

[101] For an excellent examination of the various factors at play in the creation of the Roswell mythology, see Benson Saler, Charles Albert Ziegler and Charles B. Moore, *UFO Crash at Roswell: The Genesis of a Modern Myth* (Smithsonian, 1997).

[102] Andrew Siddons, "Visitors From Outer Space, Real or Not, Are Focus of Discussion in Washington," *New York Times*, 3 May 2013.

own purposes. This technology, exopols claim, could have by now fixed all of our problems on earth. Hunger, war, poverty, and disease – all of them could have been done away with. The exopolitics movement, building from the Roswell Incident as "year zero," promotes a vision of a crushed past – a history which never happened.[103]

Much like Marx's specter of Communism haunting Europe in the 1840s, Roswell is the exopolitical specter haunting ufology, hovering like a vulture over the ruined postindustrial cities of the west and the shabby, dangerous industrial-present cities of the east, its promoters promising a global revolution of technology and knowledge.

This exopolitical/conspiratorial narrative, which began to penetrate the cultural consciousness through the work of men like John Lear and William Cooper, and then was reshaped in the first decade of the 21st century by the likes of Greer and Bassett, is just one aspect of the fascinatingly frustrating world of Roswell.

I can roll my eyes at it all, write around it and proclaim that it's not germane to my argument, but in the end I can't escape the reality that Roswell matters, if for no other reason than that the consensus reality of the UFO world says it does.

So, if Roswell isn't going away, what do we do with it? Do we pore over witness testimony until the end of time?

---

[103] One of the most prevalent recurring themes is that the government has the knowledge, gained by "reverse engineering" alien technology, to provide free energy to everyone on the planet but has conspired with oil companies and other capitalist interests to withhold that knowledge. See, for example, Theodore C. Loder, "ET Contact: The Implications for Post Contact Advancements in Science and Technology," paper presented at the July 2011 MUFON Conference, Los Angeles, CA, http://goo.gl/yCbe5d.

Do we accept the exopolitical ghosts haunting our crippled present and pine for shiny alien-fueled futures which never materialized?

No.

We take Roswell and we bend it to our dark and horrible purposes (because, dear reader, we are dark and horrible – we dare question the UFO gospel of crashed saucers, abductions, and cover-ups. We're bad people, you and I). Most of all, we have fun with it and explore the opportunities it presents for experimental thought.

In 2005, *Fate* magazine, long a stalwart in the paranormal publishing world, published *The Best of Roswell*, a collection of significant articles on the incident. Unsurprisingly, most of these were by well-known proponents of the standard ET saucer crash retrieval narrative like Kevin Randle and Stanton Friedman.

Other views, however, also appeared, from John Keel, who advocated a solution to the Roswell question which credited Japanese Fugo balloons as the "mysterious craft," to Nick Redfern, whose *Body Snatchers in the Desert: The Horrible Truth at the Heart of the Roswell Story* asserted that the Roswell crash was the result of a failed high altitude balloon experiment.[104]

The bodies witnesses claimed were present at the crash site, Redfern argued, were the corpses of captured Japanese prisoners of war, and the flying saucer story promulgated by Roswell personnel was a cover designed to distract attention away from the experiment. The story, on its face, seems at least as plausible as one involving aliens, which is probably damning it with the faintest of praise. The political

---

[104] John Keel, "Beyond the Known," *Fate Magazine*, March 1990; Nick Redfern, *Body Snatchers in the Desert: The Horrible Truth at the Heart of the Roswell Story* (Paraview Pocket Books, 2005).

and cultural implications of such an explanation are also fascinating to consider.

As a counterpoint to Redfern's controversial thesis, Randle questioned the credibility of Redfern's anonymous sources and contended that:

> Roswell was not some rogue experiment using deformed and mutated Japanese captives, but the crash of an alien spacecraft. Those who were there would have recognized everything as terrestrial if that's what it was. The only answer that takes all the evidence into account is that this was truly something from another world.[105]

I am not entirely sure all the evidence surrounding the Roswell incident *should* be taken into account, however. Eyewitness testimony is notoriously uncertain, and eyewitness testimony given decades after the event must be even more tenuous.[106] Even if everyone involved was (a) telling the truth and (b) not delusional, I believe that more down-to-earth explanations are more likely to be true.

In 2005, Walter Bosley, writing as E. A. Guest in *Fate*, told the story of his father's experiences in the United States Air Force. According to Bosley's narrative, the

[105] Kevin D. Randle, "Roswell Explained – Again," in *The Best of Roswell: From the Files of FATE Magazine* (Galde Press, 2007), 215.

[106] See, for example: Elizabeth Loftus, "The Fiction of Memory," *TED Talks*, June 2013, http://goo.gl/hckuuZ; Laura Engelhardt, "The Problem With Eyewitness Testimony: Commentary on a talk by George Fisher and Barbara Tversky," *Stanford Journal of Legal Studies* 1, no. 1 (December 1999), 25 – 29, http://goo.gl/lM4ZIW.

crashed vehicles from Roswell:

> ... came from inside the planet. The
> civilization to which the crewmen belonged
> exists in a vast, underground system of caverns
> and tunnels beneath the Southwest and is
> human. They went underground thousands of
> years ago... This is the truth about the Roswell
> Incident according to my father. A civilization
> thrives underground, hidden from the surface
> world.[107]

For some reason, ever since I first heard elements of this story it has stuck with me.[108] It may be my contrarian nature regarding the cultural dominance of Roswell, and of the entire Extraterrestrial Hypothesis, that leads me to latch on to all sorts of outlandish claims as an alternative. Or, and I think this is more likely, perhaps it is because such alternative explanations appeal to me as an historian. Finding evidence, or even proof, of a previously unknown or unacknowledged human civilization would be incredible and, professionally at least, infinitely more interesting than if the standard ET stories were conclusively proven to be true.

The notion of a hidden human society haunting our world appeals to me on a "this is very creepy and I like it" level as well. Plus, if you've read this book or have talked to me about these various paranormal-related subjects at all,

[107] E. A. Guest, "The Other Paradigm," in *The Best of Roswell: From the Files of FATE Magazine*, 201-202.

[108] It was on a 2003 episode of *Radio Misterioso* program with Walter Bosley and filmmaker Ralph Coon as guests; "Government Secrets and the Hollow Earth," hosted by Greg Bishop, *Radio Misterioso*, 1 June 2003, http://goo.gl/a8KnGE.

you'll know I'm a fan and admirer of the late Mac Tonnies, and Bosley's narrative dovetails nicely with Tonnies' speculation about a possible "cryptoterrestrial" civilization with whom we share the planet.[109]

If, in the end, Roswell is a cultural force at least as much, if not more, than it is an historical event, then it behooves us to look at all sides of it. Not *both* sides – skeptic versus believer – but *all* sides, including the ones that are *really* weird. Despite my fascination with the entire constellation of events and ideas surrounding the Roswell Incident, I tend to wonder if there's a *point* to it all.

To close, here's something I found incredibly interesting. In his introduction to *Fate's Best of Roswell* volume, exopolitics author / fellow traveler Richard M. Dolan wrote:

> Truth is not relative. It is not the luxury of responsible people to choose what to believe based on personal prejudice or whim. It is rather the obligation of free citizens to *look* for truth. Because it exists, unchanging, independent of outside forces, whether they be popular acclaim or official *diktat*... the investigation of Roswell was and remains important, not least to demonstrate that truth matters.[110]

What really interests me about this quotation is that I have come to almost the exact opposite conclusion. I believe Roswell is important because it's a crucial example of how, in the ufological world at least, narrative and story

---

[109] Tonnies, *The Cryptoterrestrials*.

[110] Richard M. Dolan, "Introduction," in *The Best of Roswell: From the Files of FATE Magazine*, xii.

trumps any notion of objective truth.

Dolan is not, as far as I can tell, a dumb guy. His *UFOs and the National Security State* was a wild and woolly trip through an alternate universe where academic history fully accepted the ufological master-narrative, even if, as I strongly suspect, Dolan was playing the thing completely straight.[111] And he's probably right – it *is* reasonable to look for the objective truth at the heart of the Roswell mystery. I'm just not entirely sure it's the most *useful* thing to do.

So with all that said, here's my takeaway from Roswell:

Stories are important.

Roswell is an important story.

I'm not sure we should look at it through any other lens.

---

[111] Dolan, *UFOs and the National Security State: Chronology of a Coverup, 1941-1973*.

CHAPTER TEN

GHOSTS, TIME & LOSS

As we walk through the towns and cities in which we live and work, the relics of the past intrude on the present and, sometimes, seem to act as a brake on the future emerging. The shapes and forms of the past, present, and incipient future overlap, compete for space and attention and, ultimately, fade from view as we walk on to the next street, the next door, the next life.

Time waits for no person; time marches on; time will tell; the time of your life. We often reduce the notion of time, and how we relate to the passage of time, to cliché status. I've heard it said that we travel in time, but only in one direction, one day at a time. I'm not entirely sure that's true (at least not true in a way that really matters). We observe time as moving forward, ticking away on our clocks, measured out on our calendars, because that's how we humans have decided to cope with a changing and decaying world.

Most of us, however, have found that we can travel backwards and sideways in time as well and, usually, we find ghosts there.

Our minds and imaginations are not necessarily bound to the same tyranny of seconds, minutes, hours and days that our bodies are. Of course most of us have to go to work, fulfill our commitments, keep our appointments; "time" makes that both possible and necessary. But what about those moments in between the ticks of the second hand, when our minds drift off to a past which was better, worse, or just different? What about the snippets of time at that meeting, where our eyes lose focus and we imagine a future so fantastically different from the banality of our present that we lose ourselves in it? And most seductive all, what about those moments when we lose ourselves to the daydreams of decisions made differently, the science fictional conceit of the parallel universe.

All of these conjure the ghosts. The eruptions of tangible history (past history, future history, worlds-that-never-were history) strike at the core of our being. They make us stop mid-breath; they confront and convict us. Like the denizens of haunted houses, even when the ghosts aren't *evil*, they are rarely pleasant. If these figures are, at least in some cases, the spirits of past residents, traumatized to the point where they cannot move on to whatever may be next, their testiness is certainly justified.

The less-than-pleasant ghosts summoned by our mental time travel have their traumas as well – traumas they've suffered and traumas they've caused. If they were at peace, ghostly conventional wisdom tells us, they would have moved only to someplace more pleasant. Too often they remind us of what we've lost: friends, family, innocence, ignorance, faith, hope, love.

I sit at my desk, writing or grading exams, or preparing a lecture, and suddenly I'm reminded of a face. It's someone I haven't thought of for years, but I'm consumed by a desire to look them up, find an email address, and drop them a note to get back in contact. Pushed by this ghost of a memory I fire up a search engine, plug in the name, and hit "go." An obituary appears and my heart turns to ice; my stomach twists and burns. I click on a link to a funeral home's online "memory book" and see *my own* words of consolation and sympathy, written years ago. The ghost dissipates and I'm left wondering how I ever could have forgotten that loss. Then I wonder why the ghost chose to arise and push me at all.

Am I just getting older?

Are my mind, memory, or concentration going?

Perhaps.

I am not entirely sure of any of this – my grasp on what happens here is as ghostly and barely tangible as the ghosts themselves.

Maybe the ghosts of the past, sleeping in our subconscious, emerge when they are in danger of being overwritten, like data on a bit of flash memory. They assert themselves, willing themselves into a kind of half-known and shadowy existence.

An eruption of tangible history.

I see future ghosts; eruptions of the possible (if not always the plausible). I look at my son and I see him as a teenager, or as an adult. In some futures, he has overcome the disabilities with which he was born. In others, he has not. Sometimes, when the rest of my family is asleep, and the night is cold and the dark close, I can see his grave, my wife's grave, my closest friends' graves, and I feel as alone as if their deaths had already occurred.

Anticipatory loss is an inoculation against the future. Perhaps the ghosts are not entirely unsympathetic to us here in present-bound meatspace. Being outside of time, perhaps these ghosts of "never were" and "might have been" and "may as well be" are giving us glimpses, preparing us for what may be coming.

And like everyone, I feel the lateral pull of sideways time, yanking my consciousness into a world where things are different. At one time, those ghosts of the other-present would have been alluring. Now, blessedly, I rarely view these other realities with envy. Sometimes, though, I indulge in the voyage to the left or right of this timeline, experiencing another life in another reality.

Ghosts of myself – micro-holidays to my summer-home in the twilit realms of fiction.

The ghosts continue to appear on our streets, in our homes, in our minds. Time will continue to march on. Losses pile up, stacked like firewood. In the end, at the moment of death, we lose ourselves, becoming the ghost in the minds of those who remain behind.

This atemporality, the blending of past, present and future in a mad jumble of confusion, is a part of us that we attempt to overcome with our notions and measurements of time. We push the ghosts to the background, but they pop up now and then. Not paranormal, by any means. Rather, they are the most *normal* thing I can imagine the human mind experiencing. When we explore haunted houses or speculate about UFO occupants being time travelers from the future, perhaps we are externalizing our own failures to control the ghosts in our minds and on our streets.

Time to relax. Time to stop *trying* to control those ghosts.

Let them rest.

Conclusion

My thoughts on the paranormal in general have changed drastically over the years, from enthusiastic believer in the "shadow government" and their underground bases to jaded academic skeptic to someone who thinks there are stranger things out there that might be beyond our understanding. This brief book was an attempt to explore that journey.

The "chaos" of the title emerges in each of the topics I discussed; describing the maelstrom of stories, personalities, agendas, impressions, data, confusion, and contradictions that inhabit the world of the paranormal. These topics are all connected but in ways that may be too big and complex for us to truly comprehend, at least at the moment.

People have tried to impose order on this chaos. Bill Cooper exemplified a trend toward the conspiratorial. The exopolitics movement does the same, on a grander, cosmic scale, tying the petty motivations of our politicians into the vast universe of interstellar life. The very basis of conspiracy theory is an attempt to find a system to explain everything – to solve every question, to tie up every loose end. Language, community, and place tie us together, but also serve as a barrier to understanding the strange, discussing it, and sharing our experiences with others around us.

The media outlets focusing on these topics have a vested interest in preserving the chaos; settled questions are much less exciting than open ones.

One imposition we all accept and live within is time itself, the linear construct we place on the world around us, using it to cope with an all too brief existence in which we age and die. Our measurements of time, in all of their varied forms, represent attempts to understand a world where the chaos of constant change and decay seems to reign. Time is the ultimate human control mechanism for something that is, in the end, uncontrollable.

In our cities and landscapes, through the ghosts that haunt them, we see even the progression of linear time break down. The old and the new overlap and, sometimes, we wonder if time is less a line and more a series of circles – cycles that repeat over and over in ways that are only occasionally visible.

Rationality often fails us in coping with the chaos. The non-rational teases us, tantalizing us with solutions that appear for a moment and then vanish. Some aspects of the paranormal and conspiratorial world are fairly straightforward to deal with – we can analyze mysterious documents that reveal THE TRUTH, and we can evaluate extraordinary claims by demanding extraordinary evidence. We can take some small comfort in our rational, Enlightenment-style epistemic bubbles.

Until, of course, we actually have an encounter that our rational minds cannot process. For some, this is an encounter with religion. For others, their moment of non-rationality is more traditionally paranormal – ghosts, flying saucers, an experience akin to abduction narratives, or perhaps something even stranger.

George Hansen, in his classic work *The Trickster and the Paranormal*, discussed the way in which the paranormal, in all its many forms, from "psi" to UFOs, plays in the liminal, borderland spaces in our world and consciousness, exploiting the gaps in our artificially constructed dualistic world. As I stated in my acknowledgements at the start of this book, I owe a lot of intellectual debts, and Hansen raised some of the general points that I applied to my particular interests here.

In concluding his book, Hansen states:

> The supernatural is irrational, but it is also real. It holds enormous power. We ignore it at our peril. It operates not only on the individual psyche, but at a collective level, influencing entire cultures... If we fail to recognized the limits of our "rational" way of thinking, we can become victims of it. Parapsychology demonstrates that our thoughts, including our unconscious thoughts, are not limited to our brains. They move of their own accord and influence the physical world.[112]

I started writing this book almost a decade after I read Hansen's work and, clearly, his ideas penetrated. Hansen, having worked in parapsychology laboratories, focuses on the psi aspects of these phenomena, but I think his ideas are applicable to any aspect of The Weird. If our unconscious thoughts are free to move about and influence the world around us, as Hansen argues, then what others besides our own might be out there, and what might they be up to?

During the process of writing these essays, I've had several experiences that I cannot explain. They're simple things, but they jump out. Things like a sudden impression (proved correct) that when I get home from work my wife will have gotten a haircut. She hadn't planned it – I didn't glimpse a calendar entry or anything. She meant it to be a surprise, and she was a bit crestfallen when I wasn't

---

[112] George P. Hansen, *The Trickster and the Paranormal*, Xlibris, 2001, 430.

shocked. She was also a bit "creeped out" when I explained my "psychic" knowledge of the haircut. Things like that, innocuous but there, have occurred with greater frequency while working on this project.

Some idle speculation: if the various paranormal manifestations and activities that surround us are connected, and if they are a conscious expression of some intelligent force, this makes sense. I engaged a part of my mind that connected to this force, waking it, tempting it to mess with me.

That's not an entirely comforting thought. In the wooded graveyard in southern Indiana, on the side of a road looking at a crop circle, or in my car suddenly *knowing* that my wife got a new haircut – in those times and places I felt uneasy. Yes, it could have all been merely in my head, but as I've said, that is just as terrifying.

We live in a weird world, which in turns inhabits a weird cosmos. Our explanations and constructs will not change that. Perhaps we should, in the end, relax and accept The Weird, even embrace it. It certainly will not go away. It exerts an enormous amount of influence over many, many people. Whether in the form of flying saucers, ghosts and hauntings, religious revelation, psychic ability or anything else, The Weird, the non-rational, the "paranormal," is not leaving us. Even if understanding it is beyond us, we may have to learn to co-exist. The attempt to come to some sort of terms with such forces may, in fact, cause us to do a better job at understanding and co-existing with ourselves. We are, after all, often as non-rational (and *irrational*) as any poltergeist or spaceman.

Which might be why they have sought us out in the first place. Maybe we are *their* Weird.

Selected Bibliography

Note: All websites were accessed as of 14 November, 2013. As is the case with citations of websites in the footnotes, many of the URLs have been shortened from the original to facilitate formatting.

Allchin, Douglas. "Pseudohistory and Pseudoscience." *Science and Education* 13, (2004): 179–195.

Barker, Gray. *Gray Barker's Book of Adamski*. Saucerian Books, 1970.

————. *Men in Black: The Secret Terror Among Us*. CreateSpace Independent Publishing Platform, 2012.

————. *The Silver Bridge: The Classic Mothman Tale*. Saucerian Books, 1970.

————. *They Knew Too Much About Flying Saucers*. New York University Books, 1956.

Bender, Albert K. *Flying Saucers and the Three Men*. Saucerian Books, 1963.

Bennett, Colin. *Looking for Orthon: The Story of George*

Adamski, the First Flying Saucer Contactee, and How He Changed the World. Cosimo Books, 2008.

Bishop, Greg. *Project Beta: The Story of Paul Bennewitz, National Security, and the Creation of a Modern UFO Myth*. Gallery Books, 2005.

Campbell, Glenn. *Area 51 Viewer's Guide*. 4th edition. Area 51 Research Center, 1995.

Cooper, Milton William. *Behold a Pale Horse*. Light Technology Publishing, 1991.

———. "MAJESTYTWELVE." *Hour of the Time*. 1997. http://goo.gl/W2IQdX.

Dizdar, Russ. *Shatter the Darkness: Confronting the Rise of Radical Evil*. http://www.shatterthedarkness.net/.

Ellis, Warren. "Being Boiled." *Warren Ellis*. 17 May 2011. http://www.warrenellis.com/?p=12772.

———. "Conversations With Things." *Warren Ellis*. 19 May 2011. http://www.warrenellis.com/?p=12780.

———. "Corpse Flightpath." *Warren Ellis*. 19 May 2011. http://www.warrenellis.com/?p=12779.

———. "The City Is There To Haunt Us." *Warren Ellis*. 18 May 2011. http://www.warrenellis.com/?p=12778.

———. "Closing Keynote." Cognitive Cities Conference. Berlin. 27 February 2011. http://goo.gl/bwjja5.

"Gray Barker Project Description." Center for Literary Computing. West Virginia University. 2008. http://goo.gl/a4f8B8.

Gulyas, Aaron John. *Extraterrestrials and the American Zeitgeist: Alien Contact Tales Since the 1950s*. McFarland, 2013.

Gurudas. *Treason: The New World Order*. Cassandra Press, 1996.

Halperin, David. "Gray Barker, the Men in Black, and North Carolina Amendment One." *The Revealer*, 13 February 2012. http://therevealer.org/archives/10430.

Joseph, Frank, ed. *Unearthing Ancient America: The Lost Sagas of Conquerors, Castaways, and Scoundrels*. New Page Books, 2008.

Kenyon, J. Douglas, ed. *Forbidden History: Prehistoric Technologies, Extraterrestrial Intervention, and the Suppressed Origins of Civilization*. Bear & Company, 2005.

Kimball, Paul Andrew. *The Other Side of Truth: The Paranormal, The Art of the Imagination, and The Human Condition*. Redstar Books, 2012.

Klarer, Elizabeth. *Beyond the Light Barrier*. Howard Timmins, 1980.

Komarek, Ed V. "1950s Contactee Movement Revisited (Part 1)." *Exopolitics: The Study of the Politics of Extraterrestrial Contact*, 11 August 2007. http://goo.gl/wuDW1o.

———. *UFO's, Exopolitics and the New World Disorder.* CreateSpace Independent Publishing Platform, 2012.

Lear, John. "The UFO Coverup." *Sacred Texts*, 15 August 1988. http://goo.gl/gKJMVE.

Lewis, James R., ed. *The Gods Have Landed.* State University of New York Press, 1995.

Lorenzen, Coral E., and James Lorenzen. *Flying Saucer Occupants.* Signet, 1967.

Moseley, James W., and Karl T. Pflock. *Shockingly Close to the Truth: Confessions of a Grave-Robbing Ufologist.* Prometheus Books, 2002.

Nebel, Long John. *The Way Out World.* Prentice-Hall, 1961.

O'Brien, Cathy, and Mark Phillips. *Trance: Formation of America.* Reality Marketing Inc, 1995.

Patton, Phil. *Dreamland: Travels Inside the Secret World of Roswell and Area 51.* Villard, 1999.

Pilkington, Mark. *Mirage Men: An Adventure into Paranoia, Espionage, Psychological Warfare, and UFOs.* Skyhorse Publishing, 2010.

Redfern, Nick. *Body Snatchers in the Desert: The Horrible Truth at the Heart of the Roswell Story.* Paraview Pocket Books, 2005.

———. *Final Events, and the Secret Government Group on*

Demonic UFOs and the Afterlife. Anomalist Books, 2010.

Schrag, Paul, and Xaviant Haze. *The Suppressed History of America: The Murder of Meriwether Lewis and the Mysterious Discoveries of the Lewis and Clark Expedition.* Bear & Company, 2011.

Scott, Peter Dale, and Jonathan Marshall. *Cocaine Politics: Drugs, Armies, and the CIA in Central America, Updated Edition.* University of California Press, 1998.

Stevens, Wendelle C., ed. *Message From the Pleiades: The Contact Notes of Eduard Billy Meier, Volume 1.* UFO Photo Archives, 1988.

————, ed. *Message from the Pleiades: Contact Notes of Eduard Billy Meier, Volume 2.* UFO Photo Archives, 1990.

Taylor, Troy. *Beyond the Grave: The History of America's Most Haunted Graveyards.* Whitechapel Productions, 2001.

Thompson, Keith. *Angels and Aliens: UFO's and the Mythic Imagination.* Ballantine Books, 1993.

Tonnies, Mac. *After the Martian Apocalypse: Extraterrestrial Artifacts and the Case for Mars Exploration.* Paraview Pocket Books, 2004.

————. *Posthuman Blues: Dispatches from a World on the Cusp of Terminal Dissolution, Vol. I.* Redstar Books, 2012.

————. *The Cryptoterrestrials: A Meditation on Indigenous Humanoids and the Aliens Among Us.* Anomalist Books, 2010.

Vallee, Jacques. *Confrontations: A Scientist's Search for Alien Contact.* Ballantine Books, 1990.

———. *Dimensions: A Casebook of Alien Contact.* Contemporary Books, 1988.

———. *Messengers of Deception: UFO Contacts and Cults.* Ronin Publishing, 1979.

———. *Revelations: Alien Contact and Human Deception.* Ballantine Books, 1991.

Wagner, C. Peter. *Dominion! How Kingdom Action Can Change the World.* Chosen, 2008.

Wanenchak, Sarah. "The Atemporality of 'Ruin Porn': The Carcass & the Ghost," *The Society Pages*, 16 May 2012. http://goo.gl/PqH89l.

Index

Civilian Agency for Joint
Intelligence (CAJI), 73 -
74
crop circles, xi, 10, 22, 25, 29 -
30, 36, 133
cryptoterrestrials, 84, 124
cryptozoology, 85, 87

D

Dark Skies, 68
Davies, Russell, 13
demonology, 50, 53
demons, xi, 35, 37, 48 - 49, 51
- 52, 54 - 56, 59, 108
Derrida, Jacques, vii, 13
"disclosure", 109 - 112
Dizdar, Russ, 49 - 50, 56 - 59,
108, 135
Doctor Who, 2, 13, 145
Dolan, Richard, vii, 71, 124 -
125
dominionism, 49, 59 - 61, 64,
81
Dreamland, 3, 87 - 88, 91, 137

E

Ecker, Don, 68
Ellis, Warren, vii, 13, 16, 135
Enoch, Book of, 55
Evangelicalism, 50, 53, 59
EVP, 4, 15
exopolitics, v, vii, xii, 9, 86, 102
- 112, 119 - 120, 124, 130,
136 - 137
extraterrestrials, 2 - 3, 37, 47,
49, 52, 67 - 68, 70 - 71, 74,
77 - 78, 83 - 84, 87 - 88, 94
- 96, 97 - 98, 103, 106 - 107,
110 - 113

*Extraterrestrials and the American
Zeitgeist*, viii, 9, 93, 95 - 96,
103, 120, 136, 145
eyewitness testimony, 122

F

Final Events, xi, 48 - 50, 138
flying saucers, 2, 7, 22, 40 - 46,
49, 73, 79, 89, 95, 100, 115,
117, 119, 121, 131, 133
Flying Saucers and the Three Men,
40 - 41, 134
Flynn, David, 54 - 55
Forrestal, James, 69 - 70, 74
Friedman, Stanton T., 67, 78 -
79, 91, 113 - 114, 116, 121
Fuhrman, Mark, 86

G

Gage, Andy, vii, 31 - 32
Gage, Shelly, vii, 31 - 32
Gallix, Andrew, 13 - 14
Gebauer, Leo, 115
ghosts, iii, v, vii, x, 2, 6 - 8, 10 -
19, 31 - 33, 53, 85, 97, 120,
126 - 131, 133, 139
God, 1, 36, 51 - 61, 64 - 65
Greer, Steven, 119 - 120
Gulyas, Aaron John, i - ii, viii -
xii, 94, 96, 132, 133, 136,
145
Gurudas
aka Ron Garman, 58, 136

H

Halperin, David, 40 - 41, 44,
136
Hanks, Micah, viii
Hansen, George, 6, 131 - 132

Paranet, 3, 68, 89
Paranormal Energy Detector
(PED), 24, 27 - 28
paranormal, the, vii - xii, 1 - 13,
16, 21 - 37, 42, 44 - 45, 48 -
49, 52 - 53, 58 - 59, 64 - 66,
70, 72, 74 - 75, 83, 85 - 91,
102, 104, 118, 121, 123, 129
- 133
Parsons, Jack, 48
Pflock, Karl, 46, 137
Pilkington, Mark, 5, 137
Podesta, John, 110
Project Blue Beam, 79
Project Josiah, 56
"Protocols of the Elders of
Zion", 75, 79

R

Randle, Kevin D., 121 - 122
Redfern, Nick, v, viii - xii, 48 -
50, 121 - 122, 137
religion, 11, 34, 52, 59, 62, 64 -
65, 79, 93, 131
Rendlesham UFO Incident,
100, 117 - 118
Rense, Jeff, 58, 89 - 90
REX 84, 71 - 72, 81 - 82
Robbins, Peter, 70
Roswell, v, x - xi, 4, 7, 9, 43,
45, 67, 90, 100, 113 - 125,
137
    fugo balloon explanation,
    121

S

Salla, Michael, 102 - 103, 107,
110
Satanism, 36, 50, 57 - 61
Saucer Smear, 45

Scully, Frank, 115
secret underground bases, 4 - 5
Shades of Gray, 39
Shandera, Jaime, 67, 78
Shockingly Close to the Truth, 46,
137
Smith, Wilbert, 97
Space Brothers, 52, 97, 104
Specters of Marx, 13
spiritual warfare, 50 - 51, 56,
59 - 60, 64
Star Trek, 2, 79, 104, 106, 113
Stepp Cemetery, 31 - 37
Stevens, Wendelle, 93 - 94
Straith letter hoax, 47
Strieber, Whitley, 44, 89, 117
Sugden, Roger, 29 - 30

T

talk radio, 92
Taylor, Troy, 31 - 32
The Hour of the Time, 80
The Saucerian, 43
The Silver Bridge, 43, 134
The X-Files, 2, 68, 90, 110
theocracy, 49, 64
Theodosius I, Emperor, 62
theonomy, 64
*They Knew Too Much About
Flying Saucers*, 40, 42 - 43,
134
time, 126 - 129, 131
Tonnies, Mac, viii, 5, 21, 83 -
86, 92, 123 - 124, 138
Tuella, 104
Two Cities, doctrine of, 64

U

V

W

About the Author

Aaron John Gulyas is the author of many history education and scholarly popular culture resources, as well as the books *Extraterrestrials and the American Zeitgeist: Alien Contact Tales since the 1950s, Conspiracy Theories: the Roots, Themes and Propagation of Paranoid Political and Cultural Narratives, The Paranormal and the Paranoid: Conspiratorial Science Fiction Television*, and *In Fandom's Shadow: Being a Doctor Who Fan from the 1990s to Today.*

Gulyas received his BA in History from Hanover College in 1998, and an MA in United States History from Indiana University-Indianapolis in 2003. He has been an associate professor of History at Mott Community College since 2006. He has presented numerous scholarly papers at conferences for a number of organizations, including the American Culture Association, the Popular Culture Association, and the Educational Technology Organization of Michigan. A card-carrying netizen, he maintains a website called *History, Teaching and the Strange* at ajgulyas.com, and is on Twitter as @firkon, where he can often be found pontificating about which version of *Doctor Who* is the best.

Gulyas lives near Flint, Michigan, with his wife and son.

Made in the USA
Middletown, DE
01 November 2023

41805875R00091